[re]designing WORSHIP

CREATING POWERFUL GOD EXPERIENCES

D0167697

KIM MILLER

Abingdon Press
Nashville

[RE]DESIGNING WORSHIP
CREATING POWERFUL GOD EXPERIENCES

Copyright © 2009 Kim Miller

This book is printed on acid-free paper.

Library of Congress Cataloging-in-Publication Data

Miller, Kim, 1956-
Redesigning worship : creating powerful God experiences / Kim Miller.
   p. cm.
ISBN 978-1-4267-0011-8 (pbk. : alk. paper)
1. Worship. I. Title.

BV10.3.M55 2009
264—dc22

2009004419

09 10 11 12 13 14 15 16 17 18—10 9 8 7 6 5 4 3 2 1

MANUFACTURED IN THE UNITED STATES OF AMERICA

CONTENTS

INTRODUCTION

Be daring, be different, be impractical, be anything that will assert creative vision against the play-it-safers, the creatures of the commonplace, the slaves of the ordinary.
—Sir Cecil Beaton,
The Secret of How to Startle

I've always had worship dreams. I began attending church when I was in sixth grade, at the invitation of my older sister. Even while sitting in worship at that age, I never could keep myself from dreaming about how it *could* be. Ways we could *do it better*. Dramas that could illustrate the point using real situations from everyday life. Ideas for connecting people more effectively.

I have lived these dreams as a part of the worship design team here at Ginghamsburg, a United Methodist church in Tipp City, Ohio, since 1995. I was experienced in drama and fairly good at recruiting. (I solicited the services of my family and friends, and assured them they would be great on stage!) These skills would serve me well for my initial assignment: to write a drama for the first Welcome Weekend in our then new building.

The majority of my work on the team in those early days was writing dramas based on popular culture. *The Brady Bunch* became *The Broody Bunch Goes to Church*, the *Saturday Night Live* cheerleaders made frequent appearances on our stage, and *Live with Regis and Kathie Lee* became *Travis and Chatty Lee with Morning Latte*. I loved the work and discovered that I was totally energized by reaching people turned off or out by traditional church.

What I wasn't good at was staying home on worship design team day. I had this habit of coming back—even though I was unpaid for my first years on the team. I was told not to think of it as a "real job," for it would never be a paying gig. One summer after coming home from a long vacation, I was told I could certainly still have this "job" because no one else had asked for it or wanted it!

After sticking around for a long time, I finally got a small cubby of my own. When I just wouldn't go away, my persistence paid off. I got "promoted" to half-time and then full-time, and eventually, I was named team leader. I highly recommend the persistence method as a way of starting a creative career. It keeps you humble and makes a great story. Even Steven Spielberg required persistence to jump-start his career. In his early years in Hollywood, he set up his own rickety desk in a corner of Universal Studios and just pretended he was employed there. He worked hard at whatever he could find to do until one day the folks at Universal decided he just *had* to stay.

Like Spielberg and others, I just *had* to stay. Day after day, the desire to connect people to God through worship drew me back. At Ginghamsburg, we refer to these worship connections as "God experiences." God experiences vary in nature, but people must have them in order to know love and hope, direction and meaning for life. Adam and Eve encountered God after eating the forbidden fruit (Genesis 3). Abraham heard a word from God just as the ax was to come down on his son Isaac (Genesis 22). Moses experienced God calling to him from a flaming bush (Exodus 3-4). David had a heart-wrenching God experience as he repented of his own deep sin (Psalm 51).

I want to believe that it is possible for postmodern pilgrims to have powerful God experiences as well. Although worship designers cannot *make* that happen in the context of our weekly worship celebrations, we can certainly *prepare* the place where God can powerfully show up. Through the use of video, music, and graphic and visual arts, we can create environments that stimulate all the senses to focus on God in worship. Then we can step back and allow the Holy Spirit to move—to do God's best work in the lives of real people. That's my dream.

As a worship designer, I have made this my mission statement: "to connect people to Jesus in creative ways" within the context of weekly worship. My experience has been that the weekly worship celebration is

- the best place for fallen people to encounter a redeemer God,
- the best environment for community connection,
- the best format to set new direction for a faith movement,

- the best atmosphere to review core values of a faith commnity, and
- the best opportunity to introduce lost sheep to the loving Shepherd.

Luke's Gospel describes the relationship between lost sheep and Jesus, the Good Shepherd, this way: "Suppose one of you has a hundred sheep and loses one of them. Does he not leave the ninety-nine in the open country and go after the lost sheep until he finds it?" (Luke 15:4).

At Ginghamsburg, we still faithfully feed the ninety-nine sheep, but like Jesus, our Good Shepherd, we are always looking for the one. Searching for sheep in a postmodern culture is something that intrigues me, as I trust it does you. As we design our worship, we strive to create wonderful and imaginative worship experiences that will entice the one lost sheep back into the fold.

And in my wildest dreams, it *will* happen! Connecting broken people to an experience of God is not a mission for those who seek a comfortable life or a predictable vocation. Designing powerful worship events for postmodern people is crazy. It's messy; it's inconvenient; it's costly. But when the one lost sheep comes skipping back into the pen, it all seems worth it.

> *The future belongs to those*
> *who believe in the beauty*
> *of their dreams.*
> *—Eleanor*
> *Roosevelt*

What are *your* wildest dreams? And in those wild dreams are you effectively connecting ordinary people to an extraordinary God? Is your dream to create powerful God experiences?

As you read this book, I hope a glimpse into my wildest dreams will help you

- assemble and empower your own dynamic worship team,
- integrate music, media, and message in your weekly worship celebrations,
- expand your imagination for designing alternative worship communities,
- find strength to persevere during challenging times of ministry, and
- rekindle your passion for creating powerful God experiences.

So let's start dreaming . . .

developing . . .

designing . . .

**and
redesigning
worship!**

PART I: GETTING STARTED

*The first cut is
the deepest.*
—Cat Stevens

A s you begin the process of designing worship, you may be humbled by the enormity of the task. What if no one is willing to help? What if your budget doesn't match up with your dreams? What if your first worship event fails to inspire?

I'm here to tell you, "That's OK!" As worship designers, we must give ourselves permission to make mistakes—especially in the beginning. Writers call it the "rough draft"; in worship design, I call it "pretending" or "dreaming." Each time we begin work on a worship event at Ginghamsburg, we say, "Chances are slim that we'll get this right the first time, so let's just focus on what we can see at this point and give ourselves permission to change and improve it later on."

As the team leader, you have the job of creating an atmosphere of permission and possibility within which your team can work. Any creative project, large or small, will be best developed in this atmosphere, and worship design is no exception. As you brainstorm with your team, you'll find yourself discarding as many ideas as you keep. Initially, it may be hard to reach consensus. But as your team members work together over time, and as you entrust your mission to God's leading, your collective creativity will eventually breathe life into the worship events you dream together.

Whether you're designing a powerful worship experience, writing a book, or cleaning out the garage, getting started is half the job. In the following chapters, you'll find a road map to help you get started, including direction for

- finding team members for your worship design team,
- developing job descriptions to define your team,
- forging a strong connection with your lead pastor or speaker, and
- empowering your team to create powerful God-experiences for a church of any size.

While the task may seem overwhelming at first, we'll be on our way if we can force ourselves to go beyond *thinking* about it and begin *doing* it. So let's just do it!

CHAPTER 1

ASSEMBLING A WORSHIP DESIGN TEAM

In the middle of difficulty
lies opportunity.
—Albert Einstein

How did we start designing worship as a team at Ginghamsburg? We started in the middle of great difficulty, as I'll describe in the following pages. Through a series of perspective-shifting events, the opportunity arose to pull together a worship design team. But before there was the team, there was worship. Worship is critical to what we do here at Ginghamsburg. Our mission statement, organized around the three Cs, is

Bring seeking people into a life-Celebration of Jesus.
Grow as disciples in Cell community.
Serve out of our Call and giftedness.

Powerful worship celebrations are essential to fulfill our call to bring seeking people into the church. But what is a powerful worship celebration?

The multisensory worship style we embrace at Ginghamsburg evolved in response to a lightbulb moment. In the early 1990s, our pastor, Mike Slaughter, went to a presentation in which the speaker used computer-generated slides. Mike was struck by the potential of that technology, and a mental lightbulb came on as he realized that pictures and visual images could be a powerful way to communicate the greatest story ever told. For the church to remain effective into the future, Mike concluded, we must cease telling the story through "talking heads" alone and begin to incorporate multimedia into our worship. Mike dreamed of worship celebrations where storytelling and artistic imagery would invite worshipers to participate in the process, using their senses and powerful mental capabilities to encounter God more deeply. (See Michael Slaughter, *Out on the Edge: A Wake-up Call for Church Leaders on the Edge of the Media Reformation* [Nashville: Abingdon Press, 1998].)

Armed with this vision, Ginghamsburg moved in 1995 into a new worship facility that was media capable. But despite the media-friendly new church building, challenges arose. No one on staff knew much about the equipment. The music director had never considered what connection the music might have with visual imagery, and simply showing random pictures during a worship celebration does not effective storytelling make. Thus a primitive version of the worship design team was formed in the belief that what no one person could pull off alone, many people together might actually have a shot at.

When it comes to designing worship, teamwork is absolutely essential. If we still think we can plan the most precious hour of the week in a vacuum, shame on us! Even as worship designers, how can we think we have all the best ideas about appropriate music, drama, sermon themes, or visual imagery?

When we do have good ideas of our own, we're tempted to claim solo credit by saying, "God gives those ideas to me." Maybe so, but remember that even God is a team of three parts.

> *"Let us create human beings in our image"*
> *—Genesis 1:26, emphasis added*

A LEADER WORTH FOLLOWING

During Jesus' ministry on earth, he assembled and led a team of twelve. Twelve ordinary people with sometimes conflicting, sometimes complementary, ideas. Twelve minds working together to get the job done. And when the task was too cumbersome for twelve, he pulled out a micro-team and headed for the mountaintop.

> *"After six days Jesus took with him Peter, James and John . . . and led them up a high mountain by themselves."—Matthew 17:1*

Jesus needed his team's input. He knew that giving it deepened their understanding. Seeking his disciples' feedback, Jesus asked:

"Have you understood all this?"

"What are others saying about me?"

"Who do you say that I am?"

"Are you able to drink the cup I am about to drink?"

Sometimes the team got the message; sometimes it didn't. On one occasion, the whole team quite literally missed the boat, causing Peter nearly to drown as he tried to walk on water. Of course, Jesus caught Peter and pulled him back in the boat. But as soon as the crisis was averted, he stepped back and encouraged his team to rethink the situation: "Now, let's go over this again, guys. Why did you doubt?"

Jesus was a master leader. As you prepare to lead your team, study Jesus' example. Then ask yourself the following questions:

- How can I follow Jesus' example as a servant leader?
- How will I verify that my instructions to team members have been heard and understood?
- How will I communicate to my team members that I value their ideas?
- How will I handle situations in which team members' ideas differ from my own?
- How will I nurture each team member's giftedness to strengthen the whole team?

Jesus and his disciples were a great team. Like all great teams, they frequently bounced their ideas off one another. Worship teams can do this too. As your team develops, you'll find yourself testing everyone's ideas in order to find out if they're worth keeping (the ideas—not the people). As Kenny Rogers sang in "The Gambler," "You got to know when to hold 'em, know when to fold 'em, / Know when to walk away and know when to run." Some ideas you'll hold tightly and run with. Other ideas you'll drop immediately and run away from. And along the way somebody called the leader (perhaps that's you!) may eventually have to decide which are which. Remember that the buck stops with you, but only after you've consulted with your carefully recruited team.

PICKING THE PLAYERS

A great team requires great players. Each team member will come with unique strengths and weaknesses. However, our experience has shown that several traits are must-haves for any worship design team member. Here are my four Fs of great worship design team players:

Faith

No matter what the individual's role on the worship design team (videographer, drama writer, music director, or another position), his or her faith matters. The faith of great players must be active, vibrant, and passionate. These people must love Jesus! This kind of radical faith is described well in Michael Slaughter's *Real Followers* (Nashville: Abingdon Press, 1999).

Remember, this is the group who, along with the speaker, will help discern the best *word* from God for the weekend. It is impossible to squeeze blood out of a turnip, and it's equally impossible to squeeze faith-inspiring messages out of faith-challenged followers.

Flexibility

Let's face it, creative people are not known for their flexibility. Once we get these great ideas, we want to see them come to fruition. We love the thrill of knowing that a great worship experience developed out of *our* ideas. But when team players (or leaders, for that matter) marry their own ideas or ways of thinking, they may be hindered from finding the *best* idea. Great team players learn that while contributing an idea is good, seeing God work is *great*. And God works best when we collaborate on ideas. Teamwork, like family work, is a lot of give-and-take. It requires flexibility.

Future Picture

Unlike historians and art collectors whose job is to look back, worship design team players must always look forward. Great team players must always carry with them a picture of next week's worship, along with the motivation to find even better ways of connecting with participants. "Hey, why not?" must be their mantra. Often it will seem that change is the only constant in their lives. Therefore, team players must embrace and enjoy the next thing—the future picture.

Fit

I once heard Barbara Walters describe the team on *The View*. She noted that they could interview and "train" many different types of women to sit on that couch, but the key boiled down to *chemistry*. A great fit.

How do you find great fit? By examining how your team functions as a unit. Are your meeting times fixed or flexible? Are your existing team members on time or tardy? In meetings, do you update one another on personal or church news, or stick strictly to business? Do ideas flow freely, or do team members speak only when called upon? Each worship design team will have its own chemistry, or DNA. These characteristics make your team unique and uniquely suited to minister within your particular church setting.

Our team at Ginghamsburg is characterized by off-the-wall conversations that skip from topic to topic often without any sense of rhyme or reason. The team players have a common sense of humor. They have fun together, but also work hard. They have an almost uncanny ability to turn on a dime. When the need arises, they're able to pull together and fix their joint focus on the task at hand. Over time, they've established a comfortable intimacy level. While they lead very different lives, they all have strong enough egos to allow them to give and take compliments and criticism equally well.

At Ginghamsburg we use the Gallup StrengthsFinder tools, as found in the book *Now, Discover Your Strengths* (New York: The Free Press of Simon & Schuster, 2001), to help ensure that each team player is a good fit. The book includes a link to an online survey that identifies an individual's top five strengths and offers advice to enable individuals to use the strengths and to help team leaders manage them.

I highly recommend this resource to you and your team. Among our various Ginghamsburg teams, each of us has been able to identify and understand personal strengths as well as those of the teams of which we are a part. I've discovered the affirmation and helpful critique that each team player needs. I'm learning what kind of communication speaks best and how each player prefers to navigate change. Armed with this information, I can lead more effectively by interacting with each team member in more accommodating ways. Our team members are learning to know and respect one another as well. This is the essence of a great team. They aren't necessarily best friends, but they truly enjoy working together and have learned to trust and respect one another's strengths.

To recap, great team players are

- faithfully following Jesus,
- flexibly offering creative ideas for consideration,
- fixing their focus on the future picture, and
- finding out where they fit in.

As team leader to these key players, you paint the biggest picture you can, then watch your team take it and run. When you give assignments to team players who meet these criteria, they'll often bring back more than you asked for. They'll consistently surprise you. They'll exceed expectations. And you'll learn that you can trust them with music selections, arrangements, video pieces, graphics, and countless other details.

CHAPTER 2
FINDING GREAT TEAM PLAYERS

Come, follow me, . . .
and I will make you fishers of men.
—Jesus, Matthew 4:19

Jesus called his team members out of unexpected vocations. Fishermen, tax collectors—not exactly the power team the religious leaders expected the Messiah to assemble. Perhaps some Pharisees grumbled about being excluded. But those unlikely disciples devoted themselves to Jesus and his mission, and together they got the job done.

In this chapter you'll learn where to look (think: unlikely places) and what to look for as you assemble your own worship design team. But before I suggest how to assemble a great team, I'll make a few suggestions about how *not* to go about it. I've learned these lessons the hard way!

LESSON 1: DO NOT INVITE STAFF PERSONS SIMPLY BASED ON WORKPLACE WARDROBE

During my first day on this team, I was invited into a conference room full of pastoral staff. Most of them wore ties. One was desperately trying to learn media as a second career. The music director was present and pouting. I could have been intimidated and given up on the spot. But Mike Slaughter had a vision that I immediately connected with and embraced. Although I had never received formal training for what I envisioned could happen, it seemed that everything in my life up to that point had prepared me for this mission.

Initially, I joined the team as an occasional drama writer with a little experience as a musician or a visual designer. As our team dreams grew together, so did my passion for the cause. I worked without pay for a year and a half, then part-time for a very small salary. Eventually, I was hired full-time as team leader. The tie wearers eventually uninvited themselves to the meetings, and we began to acquire permission and direction to pursue new team players who shared the dream and demonstrated the passion and wiring to carry it out.

You may have "tie wearers" who want to have a say in your worship design. If so, gently encourage them to trust you to carry out your God-given dreams. Work hard; demonstrate your passion. If God has truly called you to this job, you'll eventually win them over.

LESSON 2: DO NOT ASSUME ALL ORDAINED CLERGY ARE PASSIONATE ABOUT THE WEEKLY WORSHIP EXPERIENCE

Just because a clergyperson has completed seminary does not mean that worship is her or his area of concentration or life passion. Your pastor may have focused his or her seminary training on discipleship, administration, counseling, or another aspect of church life. These other areas are important to the life of your church, but they probably won't directly contribute to the well-being of your worship design team.

You can tell when a person has a different passion from worship design. He grows quiet and his eyes glaze over in a design team meeting. She asks to leave early because she needs to "work on a few other things." Do yourself and these folks a favor: let them leave. Seek out like-minded people who are passionate about designing worship experiences.

LESSON 3: DO NOT INVITE PEOPLE TO JOIN YOUR TEAM JUST BECAUSE THEY AGREE WITH YOU AND YOUR IDEAS

We all like to have our ideas affirmed. But remember, we're designing the most important hour in the week. Worship participants deserve the benefit of everyone's best thoughts. In order to achieve this, your team needs people who can think for themselves and speak those thoughts out loud. In our design team meetings here at Ginghamsburg, all contributions are highly esteemed. The more, the better. Only after we've all shared our thoughts do we begin refining the focus.

From time to time we include interns in our worship design team meetings. Some interns just want to be in the room with us and do whatever we tell them to do. They aren't nearly as helpful as the interns who speak up and say, "This is how I'm thinking about what you said," or "This is what God is showing me," or "Have you ever thought about doing thus and such?" That's an attitude I can work with, because it inspires all of the team members to expand their thinking. Instead of making me feel better about myself, it makes everyone feel excited about the team.

LESSON 4: DO NOT ASSUME THAT ALL GREAT SOLO PLAYERS ARE ALSO STAR TEAM PLAYERS

It has probably happened to you. You hear a great musician perform in a worship celebration, and you find yourself thinking, *Wouldn't it be great if we could get her on our worship team?* Maybe. It's possible that a great musician may be a wealth of inspiration to the music portion of your worship experience. But the same dose of self-confidence that enabled that performer to step out on stage may cause him or her to stubbornly hold on to ideas in team meetings.

Doing well at teamwork or solo work requires different gifts. You may be lucky enough to find someone who can do both. If not, fill your team first with team players. You can invite soloists to fill meaningful roles in individual worship celebrations. Worship design is a long-term, often behind-the-scenes commitment. Your team needs players who can shine whether or not they're in the limelight.

SO WHO DOES THAT LEAVE?

A great team is made up of talented people who can spend a lot of time doing what they do best. When we've acquired new staff, paid or unpaid, we've learned to ask the "call" question: "What are you called to do? If money and time were not issues, what would you do with your life?" The people who serve on our team are absolutely passionate about worship. They are as dedicated to their area of service as they are to their day jobs (if they still have other day jobs).

By enlisting only team members who feel truly called to worship design, we've assembled a collection of mission-driven players whom we have to pressure to take vacations. Sick time can mean they make an extra trip to the bathroom during the workday. The only things sacred are family and personal recreation time—and we all set aside a weekly Sabbath for these important relationships.

So who's on the team? At Ginghamsburg, our non-tie-wearing, passionate-about-worship, not-always-agreeable, put-the-team-first anchor players include a music director, a videographer, a graphic designer, a scriptwriter-stage designer, and our weekend speaker (Mike, our lead pastor, our teaching pastor, or someone else). During my time as team leader, I filled the roles of writer and stage designer, but the leader could double in any of these named roles.

Our team is just that—a team. It is not a committee, and yes, there is a difference. The difference between a team and a committee is that teams dream, develop, and deploy—together. Committees tell other people what to do but may not hang around to see that the job gets done. On our worship team, if you're in, you're in for the duration until the job gets done.

FISHING FOR TEAM PLAYERS

When Jesus called, his team members dropped everything and followed. For the rest of us, recruiting team players is a little more work. The task may seem daunting at first, but it's really not so scary if you know where to look.

When we've needed new team players, I've used what I call the "Stop, Look, and Listen" method of recruitment. For each team member you want to recruit, first stop and think. Think about how this person

Stop, Look, & Listen

might look, think, and behave. Ask yourself, in my wildest dreams, who is this person? Years ago, shortly after seeing Bobby McFerrin on a TV special, I found myself looking for a new band leader. Unrealistic as it was, Bobby McFerrin became my ideal as I stopped to consider the kind of person we needed at the time to create a culturally diverse music ministry at Ginghamsburg. Did I really expect that we'd get Bobby McFerrin? Of course not. But in my wildest dreams we'd find a band leader with similar strengths. Stop and dream a little about what kind of person you really want and need.

Dreaming is a powerful way to move forward with our vision. Sometimes we're afraid to dream because we don't want to get excited and then have those dreams dashed when they don't come true. Quite the opposite is true, however. If we don't risk dreaming, we can never truly know and work toward a future picture. Have faith in your dreams. Dream big and write down those dreams. Entrust them to God, and ask God to make them come true.

When you've dreamed all you can dream, it's time to *look*. Look in the places where you'd expect to find the kind of person you've been dreaming of. If you're looking for an eclectic musician (as I was), try checking out bands or clubs. Do a little research and find out where they're playing the kind of music you want to hear in your church. If you're looking for a videographer, check your local film schools and TV stations. Network with others in your church and community. Who knows? The team member you seek may be hidden right in your midst.

When you think you may have found someone, then *listen*. Listen to what God is telling you to do, and obediently act on that direction. My best illustration of this comes out of a time when we were desperate for a strong female vocalist. I was pretty concerned about it and knew I had to *look* every place I could. My husband, Clark, and I were at an outdoor street fair in downtown Tipp City. A band on the street was playing a rather eclectic mix of songs, and the female vocalist said, "Turn that radio dial a little to the right, to the country station, and we'll do the next song."

It was evident that this singer had a diverse musical repertoire. At that moment, I felt my heart pounding, and I *listened* to God prod me to speak to this young woman about singing at Ginghamsburg Church. I get that feeling only every once in a while. When I do, I know I absolutely must scrape together the courage to act on the idea that God has given me or face the future left to my own pitiful devices.

Choosing the lesser of the two evils, I waited for the singer to take a break and then stepped out in obedience to what I believed was God's voice. (Remember, I had no idea if this person had any faith background at all!) Heart pounding, I complimented her style and asked if she'd ever "thought about singing in a church." She smiled and replied that she'd love to sing in a church, but that it couldn't quite pay the bills. Her smile spoke to me of her faith potential. I responded, "If I promise to 'pay your bills,' will you come and sing with us at Ginghamsburg Church sometime soon?" She said that she would. I followed up with a phone call, and she sang with us a few weeks later.

I remember that weekend, planning the music with the band-leader and the team. I told the team about a new singer I'd met and scheduled. I didn't talk it up too much; I just trusted and asked that her first song be "Worship You." That Saturday night, this vocalist walked onto center stage at the beginning of our worship celebration and delivered that song, a cappella at first, and then really wailing it with all the stops pulled out, accompanied by the band.

Needless to say, that Saturday evening our congregation had a very powerful God-experience, and that singer became a faithful part of our music ministry. I was excited that God had given us a much-needed servant. Her strong voice and passion for Jesus were gifts that blessed our church again and again.

A few months later when we needed a full-time bandleader, we discovered that our new vocalist's husband was also a professional musician. We invited him to join us and realized his amazing strengths as a human percussionist, using his entire body to create rhythm. For that season of ministry, Francis "Fran" Wyatt's uniquely diverse music and his personal mission of people restoration became powerful threads in the fabric of Ginghamsburg's mission. Oftentimes I look back and shiver to think what would have happened if I had not listened and acted on God's voice that evening in downtown Tipp City.

Finding a worship leader at a street fair? (Finding disciples in a fishing boat?) Who would have thought it could happen? To inspire your search, here are a few other unlikely sources of team players:

- interns from area television stations
- students at local colleges
- our church bulletin and subsequent networks of our congregation
- referrals from other team players
- ads we placed on www.churchstaffing.com
- ads we placed in our local newspapers

Fran brought with him a network of musicians who, whether regularly or occasionally, learned to love being a part of the Ginghamsburg band. In fact, many of our ministry servants are the best recruiters of additional servants to join in what we are seeking to do at Ginghamsburg.

Not long ago we spotted the need for a more expansive music ministry leader who could develop teams and teams of teams for our expanding campuses. Our website ad snagged the résumé of Paul Jones, who at the time owned a music composing and audio company that did work for A&E, Discovery, The History Channel, and many other tv networks. Paul's gifts for people, music, and multiplication were a natural for our setting.

It's essential to expand our thinking about where to find great team players. Concerts, schools, art shows, other churches and denominations, and the basic networking of existing team players are possible sources for the servants you need. Cast your net far and wide—you'll be surprised at the team members you might pull in.

Stop, *look*, and *listen* to find your best team players. Be bold in your dreams! Step out and explore!

ASSIMILATING YOUR CATCH

You dreamed your dreams, you cast your net (again and again, it seems), and you think you have the makings of a great team. Now what? Once you've found your team players, you'll want to solidify their roles on the team. You may have used a written job description as a guide while you were recruiting your team players. Now that everyone is on board, it's time to do a reality check. People seldom come to us in the exact packages we prescribe. With your description in one hand and a team member's résumé (formal or informal) in the other, ask yourself: How can I maximize this person's gifts? What skills is he or she missing? Are those skills somewhere else on the team? If so, where? If not, how can I help this person acquire them?

Written job descriptions are provided on the following pages for each of the core Ginghamsburg design team players described in this chapter. Use them as they are, adapt them to your setting, or reflect on them as inspiration to create unique documents as you assemble your team.

Position: CREATIVE DIRECTOR

Accountable to: Director of Ministries or Lead Pastor

Position Requirements:
- Serves as participating player on the senior management team in order to connect the church's mission and DNA to the worship experience
- Serves as leader of the worship design team
- Motivates, coordinates, and leads creative worship development, resulting in powerful worship experiences

Spiritual Qualifications:
- Professes Jesus Christ as Lord and Savior
- Is committed to personal spiritual growth and a healthy lifestyle
- Considers this position primary ministry and occupation
- Models standards and expectations of leaders within the church, including
    - Participating in a cell group
    - Living a lifestyle of tithing and generosity
    - Serving faithfully out of call and giftedness

Education/Experience:
- Proved competence, insight, and creative grasp of multiple communication forms, including spoken word, written word, music, media, and drama
- Degree in an area such as communications, theater, English, journalism, or marketing, or equivalent life experience
- Experience in theater, music, speech, and writing helpful

Skills:
- Ability to dream ahead and oversee events, environment, and worship gatherings within church ministry setting
- Ability to translate overall church DNA into various ministry environments throughout church facilities, much as an interior designer would do for a home
- Ability to work well with strategic partners to ensure maximum quality for all products, communications, and events

Position: MUSIC DIRECTOR

Accountable to: Creative Director (may be accountable to Pastor or Associate Pastor in smaller churches)

Position Requirements:
- Oversees music churchwide
- Recruits, trains, and mentors leaders for adult bands as well as student and children's ministry areas as needed
- Serves as active player on the worship design team
- Leads and connects effectively with congregation based on pastor's or leader's vision in overall weekly worship experience

Spiritual Qualifications:
- Professes Jesus Christ as Lord and Savior
- Is committed to personal spiritual growth and a healthy lifestyle
- Considers this position primary ministry and occupation
- Models standards and expectations of leaders within the church, including
  - Participating in a cell group
  - Living a lifestyle of tithing and generosity
  - Serving faithfully out of call and giftedness

Education/Experience:
- Formal training or college degree in instrumental or vocal music, or equivalent life experience
- Experience in broad variety of settings including a wide scope of musical styles

Skills:
- Musical talent and magnetic stage personality
- Ability to arrange music and use related software effectively
- Organized work habits (or ability to partner with strategic assistant)
- Effective relationship skills

Position: VIDEOGRAPHER

Accountable to: Creative Director or Operations Manager

Position Requirements:
- Casts vision and ensures churchwide media quality based on leader's vision
- Attracts, motivates, and trains teams of unpaid servants to deploy media ministry churchwide
- Serves as an active player on the worship design team
- Demonstrates ability to dream, develop, and deploy all media-related pieces for worship, conferencing, and discipleship ministry as needed
- Assesses, purchases, and cares for all media equipment churchwide

Spiritual Qualifications:
- Professes Jesus Christ as Lord and Savior
- Is committed to personal spiritual growth and a healthy lifestyle
- Considers this position primary ministry and occupation
- Models standards and expectations of leaders within the church, including
  - Participating in a cell group
  - Living a lifestyle of tithing and generosity
  - Serving faithfully out of call and giftedness

Education/Experience:
- Degree in communications, media, broadcast, or related field, or equivalent life experience
- Proficiency in all forms of media
- Proved ability to translate the gospel through media usage

Skills:
- Effectiveness as a team leader
- Effectiveness as a team player
- Passion to grow and incorporate new methods and media forms

Position: GRAPHIC ARTS SPECIALIST

Accountable to: Creative Director, Media Director, or
Operations Manager

Position Requirements:
- Works closely with key staff communicators in order to understand and translate concepts, information, and inspiration into visually effective images
- Serves as an active player on the worship design team
- Serves as a participating player on other teams (discipleship, cyber-ministry, print communications, etc.) as needed

Spiritual Qualifications:
- Professes Jesus Christ as Lord and Savior
- Is committed to personal spiritual growth and a healthy lifestyle
- Considers this position primary ministry and occupation
- Models standards and expectations of leaders within the church, including
  - Participating in a cell group
  - Living a lifestyle of tithing and generosity
  - Serving faithfully out of call and giftedness

Education/Experience:
- Bachelor's or associate's degree from graphic arts or tech school or equivalent life experience
- Proficiency in graphic arts, print, and screen
- Working knowledge of a wide variety of related software (Adobe Creative Suite, Microsoft Photo Editor, and others)
- Proved ability to translate spiritual concepts into visual images

Skills:
- Effectiveness as a team player
- Ability to use time and resources strategically
- Passion to grow and learn new methods, styles, and software
- Proved artistic talent for translating DNA of organization

CHAPTER 3

THE VITAL ROLE OF THE PASTOR-SPEAKER

It was he who gave some to be apostles,
some to be prophets,
some to be evangelists,
and some to be pastors and teachers.
—Paul, Ephesians 4:11

Isn't it fascinating that throughout the centuries of Christendom, the spoken word has remained the single, most powerful means of persuading women and men of the truth about Jesus Christ? While God uses many creative art forms to enhance and enrich these messages, we still need to hear anointed speakers convince us of the truth through the spoken word.

Jesus had a powerful gift of persuasion. People followed him into the countryside with no promise of lunch. They thronged into tiny living rooms to hear what he had to say. Seekers were known to lower friends through roofs, reach out to grab at Jesus' tunic, and even climb trees just to see and hear him. Luke 4:32 states, "They were amazed at this teaching, because his message had authority."

Deep down, we all want to be changed—to have our hurts healed, our issues resolved, and our lives have meaning. Perhaps that is why we still gather to listen for the voice of God in the moments of the weekend message. We long for a word that will move our hearts and change our lives, and someone has to introduce everyone involved to that Source of all creativity, the Center of our existence. Someone has to bring the word of God into each worship celebration's message, and that "someone" is usually the pastor or speaker.

> *The Word became flesh and made his*
> *dwelling among us.*
> *—John 1:14*

THE WORD AMONG US

Each week as we design powerful worship experiences, I'm convinced that we are truly making space for the Word to come and dwell among us. At Ginghamsburg, that means one person must translate that Word into *words* for the team. The team can suggest points, titles, additional scripture, stories, songs, dramas, and metaphors, but the Word must be central for transformation to occur in the lives of those present and listening.

Mike Slaughter is our primary teacher at Ginghamsburg. Mike is not known for being easy, predictable, overly friendly, or adaptable. He is more prophet than organizational genius and can occasionally infuriate his teammates (prophets often forget to check the popularity polls!), yet Mike is a passionate team player. At 10:00 each Wednesday morning the team can count on him to show up in the "war room" with his Bible and yellow pad, ready to share the word from God with those around the table.

The word Mike brings isn't just a little piece of Scripture or a few ideas for points. This "word" is a life-changing, huge, hairy, audacious premise based in Scripture that, when drawn out to its full extent, will transform its hearers. Participants who experience this word will commit to being passionate Jesus followers or be exposed as religious pretenders. As we "chew on" this word together as a team, the message inside must hook us, intrigue us, provoke us, and motivate us. If there is no tension with the message, the team doesn't feel it's worship worthy.

In 2 Timothy 4:2, Paul charges Timothy, "Preach the Word; be prepared in season and out of season; correct, rebuke and encourage—with great patience and careful instruction." As our lead teacher, Mike takes this exhortation very seriously, and so does the rest of our team. Ephesians 6:17 refers to God's word as "the sword of the Spirit." At Ginghamsburg, we are fully aware that God's word will pierce the hearts and souls of worship participants. It will convict them and spur them on to follow Jesus in exciting and powerful ways. No matter what the theme or occasion for the worship gathering, the word must drive the worship. Everything else we do must support and enhance it.

Debbie Kasper, a Lutheran clergyperson and fellow worship designer, visited Ginghamsburg to observe our worship design team process. I asked Debbie to share her feedback with me after she returned home. I was interested in what her "fresh eyes" might observe about our worship environment and overall design process. Here's what she had to say about Mike's teaching:

> I was taken with the preparedness of the sermon by Friday. So many pastors are still writing on Friday. I was impressed with the level of detail Mike had by then. I also felt the sermon walk-through on Saturday was critical considering the amount of detailing you do for the stories.
>
> Mike is a very inspirational preacher. He's interesting in that he is a cross between boomer and postmodern in his preaching style. Boomer in two ways: the three-point sermon and the speaker as leader in providing answers to life's problems. (For most postmoderns, the speaker is a fellow journeyer, asking questions more than giving answers, offering options. Neither is better than the other, just different styles.) He is postmodern in his storytelling capabilities and his relational presence on stage. His delivery style is extremely likeable, friendly and authentic.

Churches will take on the passion, DNA, and initiatives of their leaders. Ginghamsburg strives to be an authentic, culturally diverse community producing radical followers of Jesus Christ. We identify ourselves as a *mission-driven* church, realizing that we will most naturally attract people prepared to bypass religious trappings in order to make a difference in the world. This is our call from God as identified through Mike as our lead pastor. The weekend messages are simply the most effective way to present the vision and give clarity to the mission. That is why the role of the pastor-speaker is vital to the design process. We *become* these messages.

MESSAGES W A MESSENGER?

There are always a number of weekends each year that neither Mike nor our teaching pastor is involved in worship as a speaker. On these weekends, we must find the messenger so the message can find us! To fill in the gaps, we schedule a variety of speakers, some from within Ginghamsburg and others from the larger faith community. The key is that we never ask someone whom we doubt will bring a powerful word from God to us.

Each speaker must share his or her word Wednesday morning, whether by phone, fax, e-mail attachment, or in person. The team "pushes" the word, even in the speaker's absence if need be, until the word seems powerful. Having a change of speakers allows for greater diversity and creative opportunities, which serves our mission well. We love the guest speakers and the fresh word they bring, and the occasional changeup allows us to appreciate Mike even more when he returns.

We are so blessed to have Mike's intimate involvement with our team. My heart goes out to those worship teams who must soldier on without this strong level of support, for deep down I know that God works best through committed leadership. Every time I make a presentation at a worship conference, it seems that at least one person will privately share his or her discouragement over the pastor's lack of involvement. These people are passionate about worship, they tell me, and deeply desire that God will move in their church community. But the pastor refuses to meet with the team or comes to the worship team meetings unprepared. What to do?

I tell these folks to talk to their pastors and assure them that they aren't trying to take over the worship experience. I encourage them to affirm the ultimate importance of the pastor's spoken word. I suggest that they share their vision for worship, where the word guides the pastor and worship team to work together to create God experiences that engage participants fully. When approached with humility and grace, many pastors will catch the vision and come around.

It's possible, however, that the pastor will refuse. If I found myself in that situation, I would pray hard and seek God's direction, but not give up on my God-given worship dreams. I know deep down that I've been wired to serve where my passions and abilities are embraced, and I would continue to pray and move toward that end— even if it meant finding another church. Life is too short to spend our best days wrestling "against flesh and blood" (Ephesians 6:12 NKJV).

The teaching and speaking aspect of the pastor's role is vital. Small word—small worship. Big word—big, huge, incredible worship! In order for this kind of synergy to take place, the pastor must stay ahead of his or her people in spirit and in truth. Mike rises at 5:30 each morning to be with God, pray, and study scriptures and related writings in order to fulfill this call. Several months after I first began serving on the design team, I boldly stated that I would stay with this mission as long as Mike stayed ahead of me. While we all bring diverse strengths to the table, Mike has demonstrated consistent spiritual strength.

SERVANT SNAPSHOT:
MIKE SLAUGHTER, MISSION-DRIVEN MESSENGER

The man who follows the crowd will usually get no further than the crowd. The man who walks alone is likely to find himself in places no one has ever been.
—Alan Ashley Pitt

Mike Slaughter has been the pastor of Ginghamsburg Church for close to three decades. When Mike first came to Ginghamsburg, it was a country church of ninety attendees that Mike quickly "grew" to sixty serious Jesus-followers. Never satisfied with collecting pew-sitters, Mike has faithfully exercised his gift of passionately communicating powerful truth through the spoken word. Listen in on this recent conversation I had with Mike.

KIM: Mike, worship has continually evolved throughout the centuries, and we've seen significant changes here in our own church in the last decade. What would you say regarding the purpose of worship as it relates to our faith journeys here at the front of the twenty-first century?

MIKE: When I think of worship I always think of two words—worship as *liturgy*, which is Latin for "the work of the people," and worship as *worth-ship*, "of highest worth." It brings us back to clarity and purpose. Deuteronomy 6:4-5 is known as the Shema: "Hear, O Israel: The LORD our God, the LORD is one. Love the LORD your God with all your heart and with all your soul and with all your strength." It's a reminder that no matter how tempted or distracted I become, worship brings us back to first worth—one God, one ultimate allegiance—and we are here to serve that one God's purpose in the world. And I am reminded that God's redemptive purpose is to get more of the church into the world rather than coaxing the world into the church.

Ironically, worship is not the central focus of the church, rather the process of *focusing* the church for God's mission in the world. Too many times Christians define themselves by that one weekly event, but Romans 12:1-2 says to offer our *bodies* as living sacrifices, so *service* must be that single act of worship.

KIM: And that is a huge part of our DNA here at Ginghamsburg Church—why we identify ourselves as *mission*-driven. Mike, what would you say have been some of your biggest learnings here in the last decade?

MIKE: One thing I've learned is that we err if, by attempting to be "seeker sensitive," we end up watering down the gospel. There will always be a limited number of people who make the decision to follow Jesus. We must show the relevance of Jesus *to* our culture but also the radical difference, the "worldview" of Jesus *in the* culture. Too often we have strived to be relevant but ceased to be revolutionary.

For instance, for the last four Advent seasons at Ginghamsburg we've explored what it means for God to come to Darfur—for Jesus to be born into war-torn Sudan. *That's* revolutionary. We bring our offerings on behalf of the children, women, and men of Sudan and challenge ourselves to live more simply that they can simply live. And we know we can't bail on this mission—it is our call from God.

Back in the 1990s, much of the progressive worship movements focused on presentation—media, drama, blending the secular into the sacred. It was meaningful to a point, yet it created an atmosphere where participation was subtly absent. *But* worship is meant to be very participatory. Last week we invited prayer requests, then all stood to say the Lord's Prayer together. This is something we weren't doing ten years ago.

For the larger church the challenge is to not fall into presentation nor to enable rote liturgy, rather to work in the tension of meaningful participation. This is crucially important as we worship together.

KIM: So what are the various components that must be present to define any gathering as a worship celebration?

MIKE: Worship components would be anything that recognizes the coming together of the saints to celebrate our relationship with God and one another. We are realizing how important relationships and community truly are. We are taking time to "pass the peace" and greet one another. Hearing others pray and praying for others create a sense of community and help us all identify within ourselves what makes us thankful.

We're seeing that faith communities will all express themselves in unique ways—emotionally as well as physically. We're experiencing various worship space configurations even among our own Ginghamsburg venues—customized worship experiences for various need-based communities.

KIM: What would you say to pastors and worship team players designing worship together?

MIKE: I would encourage pastors to work in team. One advantage of working in team is that it makes you a better preacher. Others are empowered to work with you, helping you know what does and doesn't connect. I like that right now I have four people under the age of thirty on my team, keeping me current and relevant. Working as a team is not something to be afraid of but something that makes us more effective. Creativity increases exponentially when more players become involved. One idea spurs another. That happens only when many are invited into the process and welcomed into the larger team.

One of the keys to any worship experience is moving forward in obedience to God with the fear of God, not the fear of people. Worship loses the prophetic voice of God when we fear people and not God. In another sense, we must remember that unless worship is incarnated and makes sense to the people who are participating, it's ineffective. You have to do worship based on truth and a healthy fear of God. You must have a passion to connect people using both of these together.

I'm so grateful for a lead pastor who passionately opens the written word and points us to the Living Word. Happy are the people whose God is the Lord and who have assurance that the *Word* will be incarnated uniquely each week in worship.

4 CHAPTER 4
SMALL OR START-UP CHURCHES EMPOWERING TEAMS THAT SOAR

*Without faith it is impossible
to please God.*
— Paul, Hebrews 11:6

When I have had the opportunity to speak at conferences about multisensory worship, at least one pastor or worship leader will raise a hand and ask, "If you were just starting out designing worship [whether it's because the church is small or young, or it just received a wake-up call], how would you do it?" Because the multisensory worship at Ginghamsburg is now well established, listeners just assume that it has always been that way. But we had to start somewhere. At one time, we were where they are, and we continue to refine the model. In fact, for the last sixteen years our worship center has been a research and development laboratory where we've tried at least one new thing almost every single weekend.

When I first began working on the worship design team at Ginghamsburg, the stage was large, but the worship celebration was fairly predictable. There were a welcome, prayer, scripture, and announcements; a choir sang lustily to CD track accompaniments. A couple of music lovers led a few worship songs, and Mike always delivered a great message. Despite media capability, the screen was blank the majority of the time. (My two pet peeves: blank screens and unlit candles. Both say, "The door is open, but nobody's home!")

To make things worse, the congregation, like their Israelite ancestors in faith, wanted to go back to Egypt. "Egypt" for us was our old, cramped church building where seats, parking spots, and bathroom privileges were always in short supply. Nothing felt polished, and no one felt compelled to look or sound professional. Back in Egypt, everyone could feel God's presence because we were so crowded we had to *feel* something!

But a new day was dawning at Ginghamsburg. We had reached the promised land, and a new, much larger building was ours to fill. Finding the best ways to use the new facility was a challenge—in the beginning. As Jesus noted early in his ministry, you can't put new wine into old wineskins. We still wanted to enjoy the richness of worship celebrations we'd experienced before, but we needed new wineskins to enjoy them in.

Slowly but surely, we began to think in new ways. First order of business: use the screen as a modern-day stained-glass window. We needed to get something inspirational on that screen. We continued to dream of ways we could fill up the stage, warm up the room, and enhance the space with music that inspired. What we needed was multisensory worship—multimedia that helped tell the stories and music that reflected the growing multicultural passion in our hearts. But where would we start? This is the challenge of many churches desiring to step out and start growing, and it was our challenge as well.

BEGINNING

Our dramas began with yours truly doing monologues, then asking others to join me—one talented person at a time. Our band began with a single keyboard player and gradually added drums, guitar, bass, percussion, and sometimes extra instruments. We created our first screen graphics by scanning freehand sketches or copyright-free illustrations. When we wanted to add media, we purchased a CVLI (Christian Video Licensing International) license for a modest annual fee. The CVLI license allows us to show video clips from movies, which have become an effective part of our multisensory worship. (For more information about the CVLI license, or to obtain one for your church, see www.cvli.com/.)

How do you get started? The answer for any new worship endeavor is not to scale down your dreams, but to simplify your strategy and build those dreams while you . . .

Take One Small Step at a Time

Then Peter got down out of the boat, walked on the water and came toward Jesus. But when he saw the wind, he was afraid and, beginning to sink, cried out, "Lord, save me!"
—Matthew 14:29-30

No one knew small steps better than Peter. Peter was a fragile human being with a bit of a crazy streak, but he knew enough to realize that faith can't grow in the context of comfort. As Peter and the disciples saw the ghostlike figure approaching on the water, they panicked. Was it Jesus: Or was it really a ghost?

There were only two possible outcomes to that scenario. Either it really *was* Jesus walking toward their boat, and he would eventually make it to them safe and sound—or it was a ghost, and that ghost would eventually come close enough to scare the bejeebers out of them. Either way, Peter's stepping out of the boat was not going to help! There was no good reason for him to step out of the boat that stormy night. He was safe with his buddies in the boat, and Jesus was already walking toward them. Why get out?

I think it was the child in Peter that wanted to get his own piece of the action. Perhaps Peter was a kinesthetic learner. Maybe he knew that if he could feel the power of the wind around him and the roll of the waves beneath him, he'd be onto something bigger than life. He'd experience God firsthand; he'd get a piece of the God-action. The very thought of it invigorated him. He couldn't just sit in the boat pondering what would happen—he had to get out and try it! So Peter stood up and called out to the figure in the distance, "Lord, if it's you . . . tell *me* to come to *you* on the water" (Matthew 14:28, emphasis added).

Designing powerful worship experiences in a smaller church will definitely take everyone involved out of the comfortable, dry boat and into the storm. You'll feel the wind around you and the rolling waves under you, but one day you'll be the last to leave that little church building after a powerful God experience and you'll be sure you're walking on water. As you step out in obedience to fulfill your God-given worship dreams, your faith will grow, and the faith (and possibly the size!) of your congregation will too. Remember that without faith, it's impossible to please God. Perhaps your small first step is an innovative video idea, a brand-new song, a creative theme-driven display at the entrance, or an interesting way to serve communion. Whatever that rolling wave looks like, it's important to push ourselves to take on projects and ministry endeavors that can succeed only with the help of God, with the exercise of faith.

Keep It Simple

Small churches *can* empower teams that soar. Working simple

allows for greater ministry impact using fewer people. You don't need a huge team of paid staff. You just have to cover all your bases. Start with a small team of three or four people who can cover the following key worship design team positions:

Musician

Look for a key musician who can envision, overall arrange, and perform the style(s) of music that would best enhance your church's vision and attract its target audience. (If you haven't defined a target audience, now's the time to ask your pastor and team, "What kinds of people presently attend our church, and what kinds of people are we seeking to attract?") Music is a key component in worship design. So as you begin, it's critical to match your music style(s) to the musical tastes of those most likely to be attracted to the church and its preaching style.

As you search for musicians, remember that it's easier to disciple a great musician who is new to the faith than to teach an adult disciple to make great music. The key musician on a worship team must have proved musical talent. Ideally, he or she should practice and play music regularly. Regular playing produces quality music, and it also attracts quality musicians. Musicians who play regularly know other musicians—possibly even right in your church.

Share your worship dreams with your key musician. Work together to define a musical style that will fit your church's vision and

REDESIGNING WORSHIP

mission. Then charge your key musician with the mission of building a band or music ministry out of his or her network and the church family. Encourage him or her to *start simple*, but with *high quality*. Think: if we build it (beautifully), they will come. People are attracted to that which inspires.

Technician

To succeed in multisensory worship, you'll need a technical guru who can run a projector and a sound system. "Anything is possible with duct tape," this person will confirm. The technician is a support personality who feels passionately that "if we speak with the tongues of men and angels, but have not the right equalization on the vocal mics, or the screen is dark, we are nothing."

By all means, share your vision with your technician. While a technician on the worship design team may not be required to articulate your mission, he or she should definitely understand and support it. After all, his or her skills will be critical in helping you realize it.

Word Weaver

The word weaver is someone who can grasp the message and translate it, drawing people into the experience in a variety of ways. Dramatic pieces, prayers, calls to worship, and even announcements must support the weekly word. Initially, your pastor may fill this role, but it will eventually be helpful to identify someone else who can take that load off the primary speaker and consider this a ministry in its own right. Once these pieces are outlined, any number of people can deliver them to the congregation, depending on the theme of the week.

Stage Designer

The stage designer sets both the physical stage and, perhaps more important, the spiritual stage. The physical stage includes any props, visuals, or set pieces you'll be using (for more about setting the physical stage, see chapter 8). The spiritual stage is the tone or atmosphere you're seeking to create with each unique worship celebration. The stage designer is a visual thinker who understands what it means to provide an ambience that whispers, "I have prepared a place for you . . . you are welcome here . . . the Spirit is alive and present . . . relax and be in the moment with God."

As with the preceding players I've described, the stage designer doesn't have to be a paid staff person, and elaborate stage design is not often needed. But having the right person in this position can make all the difference. Carefully placed candles, thoughtfully selected background images, and mood-setting choices of color and texture come together to draw in worshipers. The stage designer's home environment is usually confirmation of his or her passion to create spiritual spaces and an environment of expectation. It's a true God moment when a potential stage designer comes to realize that his or her gift for ambience setting can be used to advance God's kingdom.

Your Unique Team

To form a simple, small team, all you need are these four positions: musician, technician, word weaver, and stage designer. If you're lucky, you may find someone in your midst who is wired to fulfill more than one role. Or you may get "two for the price of one" and find a couple or group who would like to share responsibility for a position. Each church setting will offer its unique variety of personalities, and it's exciting to see how different churches have configured their teams. Perhaps no other church will do it quite the way you do!

Seek Only Mission-driven People

As you begin to assemble your team, resolve now to seek only mission-driven people. Worship design is not a job for those seeking prestige or comfort. These positions are for people who show up to serve because they absolutely love doing their piece. You think about paying them only when the mission requires their presence more often than their day jobs would allow and the church's

growth is such that they've generated their own salaries.

Simply put, mission-driven people faithfully and passionately fulfill their given roles not for money or prestige, or out of a sense of duty, but for the love of what they do. The ultimate desire of a mission-driven person is to see the project come to magnificent fruition—to witness changed lives and to say, "I had a part in that." Mission-driven people are real followers of Jesus, serving to make an eternal difference in their own lives and the lives of others. You need these people on your team. Real followers of Jesus are seeking meaning for their lives, a chance to truly make a difference with eternal impact.

EMPOWERING

It is the task of any paid staff to support and ensure the success of the unpaid team players. These critical, unpaid players must receive firsthand information on the message they are to enhance. They must work with reliable, focused staffers who will carry out any strategic functions that, for whatever reason, only paid persons can do.

Part of ensuring the success of any team players, whether paid or unpaid, is to be a leader in three important ways: stay in touch, communicate the vision, and connect the team members.

Stay in Touch Regularly

Schedule team meetings regularly at a mutually agreed-upon time. Most teams will meet at least weekly, but your meeting schedule should match the organizational style of your team. Whatever schedule you choose, remember that meeting times must be at the convenience of the unpaid servants, and the importance of those meetings cannot be overestimated. In addition to meetings, you may need to follow up with various team members via phone or e-mail.

Communicate the Vision Continually

Take the opportunity to paint the bigger picture as the team deals with decisions, challenges, and questions. Check in with individual team members regularly to ensure that each player understands the vision and his or her part in carrying it out. Provide opportunities for team members to do what they love to do in the context of worship development. Point the way to any additional ministry opportunities in your church or community that might help team members hone and sharpen their gifts.

Connect Team Members Creatively

No team member (including you, the leader) can do everything perfectly. We all need strategic partnerships to support us in our weakest areas. I tend to be a big-picture person. I need others around me who can provide dedicated attention to the details of a specific project. When I'm asked to design a new meeting room environment at Ginghamsburg, I always seek the help of a project manager and a second creative design partner. Encourage your team members to look first to one another, then to the larger church community to find the help they need to get the job done.

 Two are better than one, because they have a good return for their work. —Ecclesiastes 4:9

SOARING!

Once you've gathered your key players and organized them into a functioning team, you're ready to soar. To inspire you, here is a letter I received from a kindred spirit, a fellow worship designer working with a new (albeit alternative) worship celebration out of an older, established church. I asked how they were doing, and this was her response:

> Kim—We are doing really well, but the team is exhausted. No one warned us (or we didn't listen) about the volume of work that was involved, and we're all volunteers at this point. The service is growing at a steady pace (five to ten new people a week) and those that come really seem to be moved by what we are doing. As for the multisensory part, we moved the service within the building, depending on the nature of that week's worship elements. People have to come to the church on Sunday nights to find out where the service will be held that week. One week we even moved within the building during the service. It was about the Garden and submitting to God, so we actually walked through our Meditation Garden as part of the service, then ended the walk in front of an oversized wooden cross. It was really very moving, not just in the literal sense.

We have a band that moves from rock to jazz, from folk to pop to gospel. . . . We also use a great deal of drama, almost on a weekly basis. The space that we worship in changes each week too. For a communion service entitled "Gather at the Table," we actually set up tables in the worship space and had people gather and worship around them. Then we served communion to each other at the table. We've strung lights from the ceiling, draped material over all of the chairs to simulate water, and often give people a gift when they leave. The week we did "hope," we gave out bulbs. The week we talked about being where God needs you, we gave out puzzle pieces. When we spoke on money, we gave everyone a penny.

I hope this gives you an idea of what we're doing. We do one already-written service from your books [*Handbook for Multisensory Worship*, Volumes I and II, Abingdon Press, 1999, 2001] a month, and write our own the other weeks. We just completed our Advent/Christmas theme; it's about shining the light into the dark places.

Thank you for writing and for reading this whole letter. Know that you and your team are in our prayers. May God pour His richest blessings upon you and all that you work with.

Shalom—Amy

Amy's team was just starting out, all unpaid. But she moved forward with her vision, and as a result, worship participants were moved toward God. Can you sense the excitement in store for you as your worship design team takes flight?

I checked in with Amy again a year later to find out what this weekly process of creating multisensory worship has taught her and her team. This is what Amy had to say:

Kim—Thank you so much for asking about our progress; it has been quite a year. Here are the most important lessons that we have learned over the last year of doing this weekly service:

• It is going to take a lot more time and energy than you plan on it taking! In the beginning, we struggled to do just about everything. As we gained some experience, we were able to do things better.

• It is going to cost more money than you planned on. We've been struggling with money from the beginning and will most likely continue to in the future because we have really big dreams . . . and they cost money.

• An organizational plan is everything. Each service is planned over a four-week period; at any given time, the team should know where the service is within the planning phase.

• You have to be flexible! Twice in the last year we've decided a few days before the service that we needed to comment on something that was happening (in the culture) right then. We needed to write a service in a few days, which was more difficult, but we produced some of our best services because of it.

• Thank people for their time and effort. Whether it is a lay preacher that we have for one week, the service host, or one of the technicians everyone is thanked for their time and effort.

• If you are going to go out there with your worship, you have to be prepared to fail. We've been highly experimental with our worship, and sometimes it's been really wonderful. There was a time when the whole congregation gathered around the children that were being baptized and sang "Jesus Loves Me." The family joined as a whole to show that we all share in the responsibility of raising the children. But it can also be really bad—like when we were trying to have people light candles before communion. They just did not know where to go, and we ended up with a big pile of people.

• God brought us all together in this time and in this place. And for that (no matter how difficult or frustrating) we should be thankful and full of praise. This is a gift and a blessing for us all.

We have learned so much in the last year. There is a great deal of excitement, and after the summer off, we are ready to get back to work. We've made a concerted effort to do more publicity this year; advertising is important, and we are addressing the need to understand that our congregation is going to come from people who are not currently being served and from those who are outside of the current church structure.

May God bless you and keep you and your team joyful.

Shalom—Amy

Small churches and new, fledgling starts *can* empower teams that soar. There's just something crazy-exciting the first time you realize that you've created something powerful together. Take one step at a time, keep it simple, seek only mission-driven people, and be or find a leader who will support and work to ensure the success of unpaid staff. You just may find yourself walking on water!

PART II:
BEHIND THE SCENES
WITH THE WORSHIP TEAM

When I was young, I loved going over to my friends' homes and just hanging out. No matter what we did, the best part for me was getting a look inside that family, seeing how they interacted, experiencing the space they called home. I was always curious about the inside story of everyday human beings.

In much the same way, many people have expressed curiosity about the inside story of the Ginghamsburg worship team. Some have heard one of us speak at worship conferences; others have attended worship celebrations at Ginghamsburg. These inquiring minds want to see behind the scenes of our worship experience. What do our design meetings look like? How do we dream as a team?

In the next two chapters, I'll take you through a typical (if there is such a thing) week in the life of our current team. You'll get a feel for the way the players work as a team, and the way the team works within our church. We hope the following chapters will make you feel welcome at our place. Come on in, look around, and take away lots of dreams for your worship design team.

CHAPTER 5

THE ANATOMY OF A DESIGN TEAM MEETING

Nothing happens unless first a dream.
—Carl Sandburg

t's 9:15 Wednesday morning. Design team players are beginning to gather in the "war room" (which also doubles as office space for the media staff) upstairs at the Ginghamsburg main campus building. The room is about ten by ten feet, and a large round table centers the various players attending design team on that particular day—from six to ten people, depending on the week. Laptops are warming up as everyone gets wired up and ready to go.

Two of the four surrounding walls are completely covered in Plexiglas, ready for notes, ideas, lists, and schedules to be inscribed. Fresh hot coffee and water are available just down the hall. Sounds of preschool children playing float up from the worship area below, which serves as an indoor playground during the week. Regular team players, subs, and interns have come together to do what we've sought to do every week for thirteen years—design an unforgettable, powerful weekend worship experience.

Designing worship that will bring the word to our congregation is our mission, and this is where it all begins. Thus the weekly design team meeting is of the highest priority. The team leader, pastor, musician(s), media producer(s), word weaver(s), and stage designer(s) for the upcoming worship celebration must be present to design as a team. Doctor appointments must be scheduled for other days. Other ministry meetings must be at other times. To be on this team means to be at this meeting. On vacation? You can send in your replacement who has been trained to be "you" all week long. Nothing else should be planned until at least one o'clock in the afternoon on Wednesday. This meeting time is so important that there may not be a break for lunch. We've often called for delivery or given our orders and money to a designated support person to fetch lunch, which we eat there in the war room. If we took a break, we'd lose our train of thought and our momentum.

Designing worship is the best and worst part of the week. My prayers to God on Wednesday morning may range from great anxiety to wild expectancy as I prepare for what lies ahead. It's great fun to create such an event together, and yet it's very hard work to design an awesome God experience every seven days, fifty-two times a year. As draining as they might be, we're grateful for our weekly marathon meetings. Teams working with all unpaid servants have to be even *more* strategic, perhaps doing their planning on a weekday evening and possibly *not* every week. A lot of teams have to plan a month at a time or a series at a time and simply convene weekly to solidify the upcoming weekend celebration.

WARM UP

Back to the war room: the team is comfortably settling in. Closing the laptops briefly, the team is ready to focus together eye-to-eye to debrief the previous weekend's celebrations. But alas, we have already gotten off to a tangential start, discussing who saw what movie, why it was really, really bad (or really, really good), whose software needs to be updated, whose recent vacation was boring or cool, how the kids are, how the parents are, and so on. Lots of teasing and team jokes go on here. Perhaps humans need this kind of lighthearted, relaxing atmosphere when faced with daunting tasks. If our meetings were all business, the team would eventually burn out.

DEBRIEF

So after we warm up, we debrief. The team reviews the worship elements from the previous weekend (the three days that have passed since Sunday offer plenty of forgetting time!), and participants discuss what they felt worked, how the congregation connected, and whether anyone has heard reports about the experience from outside the team circle. Identifying elements with which people connected or disconnected, or elements that were distracting, is important. Our debriefing includes everything from message delivery to technical details. Listen in on a typical debriefing session:

"I liked the reader's theater in the middle of the opening song."

"I did, too, but we shouldn't do it again for a while. We've done that twice in a month's time."

"Yeah, I know. It just seemed to fit so well."

"Wonder why we go in streaks like that?"

"Speaking of streaks, all the music last weekend had a very 'white' vibe. Did you notice that?"

"No, the offering song had a Latin feel."

"True, but the worship music was way-vanilla."

"Good point. Let's be sure to work up some gospel or R & B this week. We've got a large vocal ensemble scheduled."

"Mike's message hit home for some people. I think others might have needed more definite action steps. Not everyone thinks in concepts, you know."

"Let's keep pushing the action steps part of the message then. You're right. A lot of people really want bottom line."

"*I* heard action steps!"

"Well, we can keep pushing it anyway. How was the music mix in the house?"

"Good on the floor but a little weak in the balcony. Sure wish we could afford some extra horns."

"Not a good time right now. Let's put it on the wish list."

Remember the Gallup StrengthsFinder tool I described in chapter 1? One of my top strengths is input. Although I don't *love* negative feedback, I always feel that the more we know, share, and debrief, the better positioned we'll be to improve. I'd much rather hear criticism in a positive way from a family or team member than wait for the negative criticism from someone else. We want the people in the congregation to be blessed and strengthened, so we try to discover what needs to be improved before *they* do.

After the debriefing portion of our meeting, we often take a five-minute break and then resume, ready to wrestle with the word.

WRESTLE WITH THE WORD

Mike always comes with the word, a golden nugget of truth representing a huge, powerful challenge. Mike's word may come to us complete with three points and several additional scriptures, but not necessarily. Mike simply articulates the primitive form of his yellow-pad message in the best way he can. The team takes notes.

DETERMINE THE FELT NEED

During my years at Ginghamsburg, I've learned to celebrate being fully human. I know I don't have all the answers, so I try to "stay in touch enough with my 'earthly mindedness' that I can still be of some heavenly good" (to misquote a popular phrase). Each week in our meetings team members seek to discover the felt need that is represented in any given message. They ask themselves, What is the human baggage we bring to this divine message? It's a great question to ask yourself when you're preparing a teaching of any kind.

As the felt need is discussed, the team won't agree all the time. Certainly if four thousand people come together for worship (as they do at Ginghamsburg's weekend celebrations), four thousand nuances of felt need will be represented. But we can no longer get away with pretending that people are dying to hear anything the church says just because the church is the one saying it. People no longer attend church out of loyalty or tradition. If people are willing to give us (and God) one hour of their precious weekend time, we need to do everything possible to connect with them. In other words, this had better be good, and it had better be relevant.

Even it if seems as though full agreement won't happen, the team wrestles until settling on a felt need that will draw in people, no matter how long it takes. It isn't wise to cheat or borrow from the time spent dialoguing with the speaker, wrestling with the word, and identifying the felt need. The outcome is a matter of life and death.

A few years back I visited an enormous worship celebration in an Atlanta church. They had screens and lighting that made me salivate. I turned six shades of green as I listened to the quality of the sound system. I understood every word of every song, and *all* the words of every song were displayed on the screen. The folks on the stage knew their parts. Nonetheless, I spent a lot of time reading my bulletin that hour, partly because it was the size of a small novel and partly because I could easily listen and read at the same time. Why? Because from the get-go, no one engaged my heart. No one showed me how the day's message from God might be a message I needed for my life. In fact, the first portion of the worship celebration wasn't even directly connected to the message. It was more like a warm-up act to keep us occupied before the real deal (the message itself).

This worship service had a detailed program and a beautiful atmosphere, yet no felt need had been identified. No one was asking the *why* question: "*Why* do I need this hour?" Or the *how* question: "*How* will God use this hour to transform my life?"

The church has not been known to be terribly adept at identifying felt needs of the culture and addressing them. The world calls this process marketing. Jesus called it being fishers of men. He was good at it, and the church can follow his example. Before Jesus began to teach a crowd of people, he fed their felt needs (often physical hunger). After their needs were met, they were ready to listen. We can start feeding our people's hearts and minds long before the message portion begins by considering and addressing their felt needs through songs and silence, prayer and participation, humor and hard questions, drama and digital storytelling.

Back to the war room. After about forty-five minutes, the team has identified a felt need and asks Mike if he's had enough time to dialogue with the team to develop his weekend's message. If he says yes, the team moves on. If he says no, the team asks how it can help further. Most great messages come about through some degree of angst. Identifying what God has to offer, wrestling to assess the possibilities, and then deciding how to communicate the powerful truth that ordinary people really can live extraordinary lives, under the influence of an amazing Savior.

WORKING IN SERIES

Over the span of the last several years our pastors have embraced a style of preaching in series. With input from various church leaders and staff, Mike gains a vision for where the church needs to go in a given year and maps out a basic schedule covering the majority of the year's weekends. This map usually includes one lengthy (eight-month) series, usually a book study (Nehemiah, James, etc.) that can subsequently be broken into smaller mini-series. Holidays and special events must also be factored into this schedule. This series style actually simplifies the worship planning process significantly. One powerful piece of graphic art becomes the banner ad for the whole series for posters, website, and invitation purposes. The subsequent weekly graphics can retain pieces of this same graphic look and thus avoid creating a brand-new artistic concept each and every week. The stage design can be more sophisticated and purposeful given the enduring quality of the series. Planning ahead—although never fully possible—becomes a bit easier when basic themes have been decided ahead of time. Your pastor and team might consider the series method and map out your future worship plans.

NAME THE ELEMENTS

When the team is ready to move on, members organize themselves around a simple list of elements that will give clarity to the worship celebration:

Word: The specific scripture passage

Felt need: The human issues we bring to this topic

Desired outcome: The goal the team will strive to achieve in the celebration

Theme: The title given to the weekend's message

Look: The objects, images, processes, or experiences that visually support the theme and message

After the *word* and *felt need* are established, the team determines the accomplishments to achieve through this worship celebration. What is the *desired outcome* for the weekend? What is the desired people-response? Will they pray a prayer of salvation? Decide to join a cell group? Open themselves to God's love? Writing down and clarifying outcomes together are a worthwhile exercise. We can't know if we've gotten there unless we know where we are going in the first place!

Next are the *theme* and the *look*. It's impossible to say which must be designed first, for you can't really control this part of the creative process. It works best to begin speaking out and writing ideas and pictures, certain that all will be dreamed and decided upon in time. The *look* can be especially difficult to come up with. Some weeks it takes a long time to dream up a great new way to visualize a timeless truth, yet when the team perseveres and hits on just the right look, the creative energy carries through the week. We've used motorcycles as an image to represent life's ride of faith; we've used old eight millimeter film footage to communicate leaving a legacy. Once we've agreed on the look, we build on that look to create graphics and design the stage environment that will help the message stick visually with an audience that absorbs messages with all its senses.

At times we have spent much energy hammering out the "perfect" theme, but in a sense, the theme is our marketing tool. It goes on our website. It is displayed on the screen, in the bulletin, on the message CDs, in the podcast archive, and in the message note page. It is ingrained into our congregation's brains, and that's why it deserves significant creative energy. It's like naming a child—except that six people need to agree instead of two!

The theme must be short and quickly understood. If there is any concern that people might not get it right away, the team adds a tag line for clarification. Our themes seldom describe the negative side of the message, most always naming the positive because Ginghamsburg's brand statement is *where God grows hope one life at a time.* For postmodern people, hope is huge! Here are some themes and additional elements we've used in actual worship celebrations.

Word: "God raised him from the dead . . . because it was impossible for death to keep its hold on him" (Acts 2:24).

Felt need: Resurrection is a mindset that I must first experience.

Desired outcome: To stand up and move forward in the power of the resurrection.

Theme: Resurrection . . . alive again!

Look: Butterflies and orange flowers

Word: "The Spirit you received does not make you slaves, so that you live in fear again; rather, the Spirit you received brought about your adoption to sonship. And by him we cry, 'Abba, Father.' The Spirit himself testifies with our spirit that we are God's children" (Romans 8:15-16 TNIV).

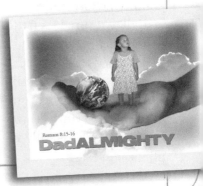

Felt need: Safety and security . . . I need the acceptance and care of a heavenly Father.

Desired outcome: To embrace and enjoy the love of the Father who loves me.

Theme: Dad Almighty

Look: Heavenly clouds with little girl standing in large God-hand a la the movie *Bruce Almighty*

Word: "Keep on loving one another as brothers and sisters. Do not forget to show hospitality to strangers, for by so doing some people have shown hospitality to angels without knowing it. Continue to remember those in prison as if you were together with them in prison, and those who are mistreated as if you yourselves were suffering" (Hebrews 13:1-3 TNIV).

"Now this was the sin of your sister Sodom: She and her daughters were arrogant, over-fed and unconcerned; they did not help the poor and needy" (Ezekiel 16:49).

Felt need: To reach out with a deeper brand of Christianity than I'm currently demonstrating.

Desired outcome: To leave my comfort zone in order to relate to the stranger.

Theme: Strangers Among Us

Look: Human walking down road, shadow is an angel

DESIGN THE STRUCTURE

With the elements set in place, the team moves on to work on the structure of the worship celebration. What music, media, drama, or other multisensory means will we use to communicate these elements in worship? The team often begins by brainstorming music, whether for the purpose of storytelling, description, or worship. Ginghamsburg has for some time embraced an extremely eclectic array of musical styles. We combine the ideas and human database of the team with computer searches for lyric keywords (see chapter 7 for more about current resource sites).

While sorting through song choices, others may go to work finding or brainstorming helpful media pieces. Team players may search the Internet for relevant video clips (www.imdb.com, www.visualworship.com, www.hollywoodjesus.com, www.wingclips.com, www.highwayvideo.com, www.avisualplanet.com, www.towardwonder.com). Final selections must communicate examples of the message in real-life form. The theme might call for a digital storytelling from the Ginghamsburg family, an authentic example of the spoken message to come. The media piece for the weekend could be an "On the Street" kind of intro to the worship celebration shot in downtown Dayton, Indianapolis, Columbus, or Cincinnati. Or the team might dream up an interactive real-life scenario that ties in to the message. For example, we used "Jump!" (my own skydiving experience) to represent Zacchaeus's faith commitment to come down out of the tree. (See Redesigning Worship Companion DVD.) Sometimes the media piece takes on a "mission moment" feeling, highlighting an exceptional ministry being carried out by church servants here at Ginghamsburg. The sky and your team's imagination are the only limits to what can be done through media. Various additional dramatic pieces are frequently considered, including

- reader's theater (a dramatic reading using one or more voices where the players are stationary but expressive),
- dramatic monologues,
- scriptures read at strategic times, or
- Bible storytellings woven into an appropriate song selection.

You'll find examples of our dramatic pieces in the appendix. As the meeting goes on, team members simply let their minds wander as they dream about what could be. "What if . . . ?" they ask. Every week's design team meeting begins as a new canvas, a blank page just begging to be filled with fresh images that convey gospel messages. "What if . . . ?"

And so, eventually as they keep writing their "brain rain" on the whiteboard, dreams emerge. A design comes through. Thoughts are clarified, and a picture of the weekend's potential begins to form. Team members are ready to go for it. "What have we got to lose?" they ask.

Jesus said, "Whoever finds his life will lose it, and whoever *loses* his life for my sake will find it" (Matthew 10:39, emphasis added). In our postmodern age, Jesus' words challenge us to lose the performance and replace it with participation, to lose the talking heads and replace them with pictures and stories, to lose the emphasis on numbers of pew-sitters and replace it with numbers of life-losers.

We haven't changed the message here at Ginghamsburg: the message has changed us. Worship celebrations have become the launching pad, the mission control tower for all other ministries. Because even in postmodernity, worship is still the place where the greatest number of real followers check in at least once a week to refocus, refuel, and refresh their spirits. The worship team owns the responsibility to make sure it happens. But it's never really just about the team and its ideas.

Worship is the culmination of lives poured out, of real stories told, of the life-changing word being pronounced. God's desire is for us to come, to worship, to change. And so, in this design team meeting, team members find agreement in the places they can. They ask for trust from one another in the places that they can't fully agree. The players take their assignments and trust that the Holy Spirit will continue to work in and through them as they leave the war room and set out to develop the weekend's worship experience.

CHAPTER 6

DEVELOPING THE WEEKEND WORSHIP EXPERIENCE

Let the beauty we love
be what we do.
—Jelaluddin Rumi

The team leader must take responsibility for assuring that as the team exits the war room, everyone carries a clear picture of what he or she is responsible for. Whatever joking and lighthearted fun has transpired in the design meeting, the team players must know they can count on one another to bring back the various pieces of the puzzle on Saturday. You cannot serve on this team and not come through. Mike once told me an organism will reject a foreign virus, that is, one that does not contribute positively to the body's functions. You can't function on this team if you need someone to hold your hand . . . period.

By Saturday afternoon, everyone will be ready. In the meantime, the team leader must keep everyone cohesive. One person may be writing a drama or other spoken pieces for the worship. Another person may be recruiting stage talent or ministry personnel as needed; someone else will oversee the design and execution of any required stage and worship area enhancement. All week long the team leader must be in dialogue with the team members, double-checking to ensure that together they will deliver all the promised pieces with grace and clarity.

Mike will have a completed message by noon on Friday. Our media producer will have storyboarded, shot, edited, and produced a classy video, or otherwise secured a relevant film clip. The graphic artist will have created, critiqued, and re-created the weekend main graphic, the message graphics, the song graphics, and the weekend update graphics. Our weekend servants will be preparing themselves at home by checking the music and media ministry boards on our website for where and when they'll be serving. The music team leaders will have arranged and rearranged, rehearsed and reworked the weekend's music.

A WEEK IN THE LIFE OF THE TEAM

Because each of the worship pieces is unique, no two weekly processes are identical. Each of the team players considers his or her work to be art, and art is not necessarily a structured endeavor. They add a little here, take away something there, tweaking, asking for feedback, and tweaking some more. It's a very intuitive process, but it works because the players are able to constantly stay in touch with one another, with the weekly word, and with the agreed-upon felt need. That's how it is possible to reconvene on the weekend and integrate these individual pieces into one powerful worship experience.

Your team may require a different schedule from ours, especially if it is mostly made up of unpaid servants, or if you aren't able to meet on a weekly basis. Nonetheless, walking through the Ginghamsburg worship team's schedule will give you an idea of how all the pieces come together for a weekend worship.

Welcome to Wednesdays

While it's difficult to nail down the *specifics* of what the team does throughout the week, it is possible to describe the *types* of tasks each one does day to day. In chapter 5, I outlined the anatomy of the Wednesday design team meeting. The worship planning always begins on Wednesdays, but it doesn't end there. Team players may need to touch base with one another, confirming, "Now we did say we wanted to use warm sepia tones in the main graphic this week, right?" or "Are we sure we'll have a guest saxophone player stage, right?" Once the team leaves the war room, reality sinks in, and the players may find themselves with questions they hadn't thought of before. To make sure everyone stays on the same page, someone always carefully copies the plans off the whiteboard. By workday's end Wednesday, the plans have been typed into a rough-draft script.

Wednesdays are also for thinking through who else might be needed for this worship experience. Because the plans are made so close to the weekend, any additional personnel must be contacted by Wednesday night in order to have the best chance of securing their services. Our media producer will attempt to reach the people he needs for the shoot ASAP to schedule the best time for that to happen. The same goes for any unforeseen dramatic or musical talent that may be required.

As contact is made with these people, it is important to recognize that we may be putting them in a tight spot. For the team, timing is critical, and unpaid servants may have to change their schedules if they want to participate. Sometimes an explanation about how we work "in the week" helps these servants weigh the benefits of participating against the realities of their schedules. If they have experienced our worship, they usually understand and appreciate the benefits of in-the-moment ministry. (Our worship teachings and themes are known for being very relevant to real life–right here, right now!) Most of the time the team and servants figure out a way to make it work.

Ideally, by 6:00 p.m. Wednesday, any extra weekend musicians have been notified regarding the need for their particular talent for the upcoming weekend. Drama players have been contacted and secured, visual components for the main graphic have been found, and a video shoot has been scheduled (key word here: *ideally!*).

Each team player has a good idea of what must be accomplished each day in order to be ready when the weekend rolls around. Everyone has daily and weekly to-do lists, which you'll find outlined at the end of this chapter. Once the players feel they have a good grip on the worship celebration, they blend into congregational life at Ginghamsburg by giving their gifts and time to various other ministry endeavors when possible.

Wednesday night is a huge discipleship class night at Ginghamsburg. Each week we set up tables and chairs to transform our worship area into a food court with full adult and children's menus. The media team simply makes sure that the ambience is right. Most times the menu reflects a different nationality or culture. Mexican night, German fare, soul food–you get the idea. Screen graphics from the weekend updates scroll continuously, and there is music that may fit the theme as well.

The food court offers a convenient way for church members to feed their families for a modest price (kids under ten eat free!) and, perhaps more important, encourages them to come as a family for classes, events, and learning groups at every age level. The worship team enjoys the fellowship with the larger body. After eating at the food court with family, the team still has a bit of time to take care of an assortment of details related to worship: doing research on the Internet, writing or shooting video for the weekend, refining a drama script, meeting with vocalists, and so on.

Mike does not usually work further on the message Wednesday. Instead, he spends his day connecting with other ministry leaders or tackling various responsibilities. He may teach a class or mingle in the food court to touch base with our people.

Thankful for Thursdays

Thursday is a great workday for the worship design team. Staff chapel at noon is the only ongoing mandatory meeting for the team–and a good time to touch base over a delicious two-dollar lunch. Before and after chapel, the team is generally free to work on worship pieces. The media team will be working on the video shoot–on the Ginghamsburg campus in a makeshift studio or occasionally as far away as Indianapolis. Once the shooting has taken place, the media producer will come back to the office and begin the long, arduous process of capturing and storyboarding his video. This process takes twenty-five hours on average and requires artistic thought, concentration, and perseverance. It would be fairly normal for the media producer to work until 7:00 or 8:00 p.m. Thursday at the church, then take work home to do more editing that night.

The graphic artist will be creating and tweaking a main graphic as well as a coordinating artistic animation loop that runs under the song text during the weekend song celebration. Currently, our graphic artist also produces a fun, shorter weekly video to lift up a Ginghamsburg mission or ministry during the update portion of the weekend celebrations. This piece becomes a commercial break of sorts, and it has truly engaged our congregation as it highlights the wide variety of mission movement going on in and through the Ginghamsburg community. "Money follows mission" is one of the mantras you're likely to hear in and around Ginghamsburg, and the proof is in the offerings. Lift up the mission, and God's provision faithfully follows.

Thursday our music director wears his arranger hat. We do not purchase written music, but arrange or rearrange our own, often using the resources offered through various worship music companies. Currently, our music is arranged using Logic Studio or Finale software, always with a healthy dose of the Ginghamsburg flavor mixed in. On Thursdays our music director may take time to have breakfast or coffee with a fellow musician or meet/audition someone from the community who wants to know more about what Ginghamsburg does musically. He might connect with others on the team to assure their pieces will line up with the music. The team is keenly aware of our need for strategic partners in ministry and often takes time to just sit and talk to brainstorm old challenges or new ideas.

By 6:30 p.m. Thursday, the weekend band has arrived and is setting up, as are the weekend vocalists, whether a choir or smaller team of singer-servants. They have a preliminary rehearsal, going over the high points so that musicians can effectively practice on their own before coming back together on Saturday. Thursday is an arts night of sorts at the Ginghamsburg main campus building, allowing multiple music groups, bands, and choirs to rehearse without worrying that their sound might disrupt discipleship classes, which are scheduled for other buildings or times. Thursday evenings are also children's choir rehearsal nights. The children's choirs are strategic to our ministry because (1) kids love to sing in "big" worship (about five to six times a year) and (2) it presents a great opportunity to invite parents, grandparents, and friends into our worship celebrations.

Meanwhile, the team is still at work on the scripts, the videos, the message, and the music. When we use Thursday to think through the upcoming celebration, Fridays go a lot better. Even in the best weeks, however, final details come together in the slightly chaotic atmosphere of . . .

Freaky Fridays

Fridays are chaotic and crazy in most organizations, but I think our freaky Fridays–with all we're attempting to accomplish–offer the potential for stress on steroids, albeit fun stress, if there is such a thing. Rather than just designing their individual worship pieces, team players are beginning to share their designs with one another, and it's tough to miss the excitement of the work that's emerging. I've often found myself *humming* the music that's been chosen. The weekend graphic is lookin' good, and the stage is being styled in yet another awesome way. Mike's message is taking on significance of its own, and the prayer written to lead into it is just right. The freakiness comes in the chaotic busyness of bulletins being completed in time to go to the printer, weekend classrooms being prepared, equipment being set up, stages being set, food being cooked, and messages being completed. Most would love working in this atmosphere of excitement and urgency. Something good is about to happen here!

On Friday morning, there will still be major work to be completed on the video pieces for the weekend, but the unpaid weekend media crew is ready to go. If the design team has chosen a video clip from a movie, the team usually verifies together exactly where the start and stop cues will take place. The music has also been rehearsed, but Friday morning the song text must be proofed and reproofed to allow for the least number of distractions possible on the weekend. Dramas have been rehearsed, messages reworked, and the final draft of the technical script is in the printer. The team is *almost* there . . . but not quite.

At 11:00 a.m. Friday all individual work ceases for the second most important meeting of the week: micro-team. It's when the team reconvenes to hear the final draft of Mike's message. Since the worship celebration is wrapped around this message and theme, the entire worship team has gathered to hear the message and make the necessary connections to his or her artistic weekend pieces.

Just as in the Wednesday design team meetings, micro-team meetings are a combination of lighthearted fun, safe space for challenging issues, and the nitty-gritty of dreaming the imagery that will best enhance the weekend's message (you can check out our message graphics on the website: www.ginghamsburgglobal.org.).

Much thought goes into making these visual communication pieces clear, engaging, and original. The church has traditionally underestimated the power of the human brain to absorb messages through changing visual imagery, and I like to think we're addressing that deficit as we talk through these important pieces. The team understands one another's best gift to the process, and it's a dialogue that never becomes static, week after week. The graphic designer is taking the speaker's script and marking it for graphic in-cues and out-cues. He is making a list of the graphics he needs to create, carefully marking portions of scripture for the speaker , the version of the Bible the speaker will be using, and the exact wording of the points to be displayed on the screen.

The media team is prepared to work quite late on Fridays. More than likely, our graphic artist will work past midnight on the message graphics, most of which can't be started until after micro-team and the unveiling of the final version of the weekend message. Our digital media producer will also work as long as it takes to get the video in good enough shape to allow it to "render" several hours before Saturday's message run-through. It's easy enough to find these media people Friday afternoon and evening. They're glued to their computers, side by side in the same office, full focus ahead. Their spouses understand that this grueling Friday night ritual is the nature of the Ginghamsburg worship "beast."

Our music director spends Friday attending to various details for the upcoming weekend—everything from lyric changes to key changes, a challenge that might have arisen from choir rehearsal the night before (yes, we have them too!), or perhaps helping to create the perfect music bed for the weekend video. This lead musician often leads the worship celebration conversationally, whether through presenting the call to worship or segueing worship songs together, and may prepare for that as well.

By late Friday afternoon, the music director also tries to squeeze in some downtime with his family. Saturday and Sunday will be a physical and emotional marathon for this busy servant, so he tries to take Friday evenings a little easier in order to be prepared.

After micro-team, Mike remains available to address questions about anything pertaining to his message or to the worship in general. All the worship team offices are in close physical proximity (except the music offices), something requested long ago so that the team can have an ongoing worship dialogue when needed. Mike's Friday afternoons are open for appointments and time with other staff. He may take off early to be better prepared physically for the long weekend ahead, a total of more than three solid hours of speaking time alone.

A number of people carry out less obvious but equally important administrative weekly tasks: proofing and printing scripts, then distributing them to all the weekend teams–music, media, guest services, Deaf ministry, and security. This script becomes the guide for the work of the weekend, allowing the details in the minds of the core design team to be effectively translated to address questions of every other ministry team involved with this weekend event.

In addition to the more obvious worship-related pieces, our cell ministry director attends the Friday micro-team in order to hear the message and subsequently create a set of questions to help the church family and cell groups go deeper into the issues presented. These questions appear in our weekly bulletin on the back of the printed message outline. Both pieces are posted to our website as well (see www.ginghamsburg.org/sermon/resources).

We've also created weekly checklists of meetings to connect with our campus site team, the custodians who may be counted upon to lift heavy stage set pieces and possibly set up the worship area for an increased number of people, and so on. We are quite careful to create a physical environment that will achieve the most engaging worship ambience for that particular week. Because our main stage, our seats, our balcony spaces, and our technical equipment are movable, someone must think through each worship celebration and specify the exact physical setup, from communion tables to candelabras. Different setups are required for different weekends–there is no default. So, it's imperative that we're clear on Friday about what we'll need Saturday and Sunday. If you have help from other staff or servants, you may want to create a physical list of the tasks you'll ask them to perform. (You can use the to-do lists at the end of this chapter as a starting point.) As the setup is done, the items on the list can be initialed and crossed off. In my early days at Ginghamsburg this component was a team of "me, myself, and I"—a scenario that may be similar to yours right now. It goes without saying that anyone who helps, whether staff or unpaid servant, campus site team member, friend, or spouse, is treated like a respected part of the team. Show your appreciation!

One additional detail on Friday is finalizing and posting our upcoming weekend main graphic (along with engaging text) onto the home page of our website. Letting people know what's coming up offers a sense of anticipation and excitement for TV shows, movies, and yes, worship celebrations. I know when I've planned to visit other churches, it's been beneficial to be able to log on and catch the weekend theme ahead of time. This small detail helps to change the perception of our worship celebrations from "same ol', same ol'" to an air of expectancy.

Other Friday tasks may include rehearsing a drama, deciding the gel color for the ambient lighting in the worship area (see chapter 8, "Styling the Stage"), checking in with the hospitality team to discover what will be going on in the lobby that weekend, and tracking progress on media pieces. I've always loved the variety that Fridays represent, yet it's important to find some downtime before the weekend madness begins. Those on the team who can break away are ready to do something fun and unrelated to worship, to rest and rejuvenate in preparation for the weekend ahead.

Saturday Insanity

Saturday starts out slow but gains momentum as the team moves toward worship time. In the morning, the media team may be putting the finishing touches on the videos and graphics. Musicians may be rehearsing alone. The music director may be tweaking an arrangement or setting up extra musical equipment. The person styling the stage may be gathering those pieces from home, a nearby shop, or a hardware store. I've often mentally rehearsed the worship experience to think through how the music will sound, how the stage will look, and how the transitions will feel. The weekend worship host and drama players will be going over their spoken pieces, focusing on connecting as best they can with the Ginghamsburg church family.

The general rule is to come prepared for the work and weekend ahead. By 1:30 p.m. most of the teams are on campus. The media and music personnel are already setting up cameras, checking cables and monitors, finishing up the media pieces, and rehearsing the band. Final touches are done to the stage and decisions made about where all the musicians will be placed for maximum visibility and audience connection. I call this Saturday insanity because everyone is excited *and* a bit nervous. There's always a hint of anxiety in the air because participants realize they're not quite ready. But ready or not, they have hope and expectancy that powerful moments are ahead. Humor and laughter help ease the unspoken tension as teams interact and touch base with one another.

At 2:30 p.m. Mike (or another weekend speaker) will meet with the media team, including the unpaid weekend director, gathering around a monitor in the media office to run through the message—this time with the newly created graphics on cue. With script in hand, Mike talks through his message while the graphics program is advanced. Mike makes sure that his thoughts are well articulated and that his transitions are smooth. The graphic artist simultaneously checks that all the scriptures are right and that the graphics satisfy everyone, without distraction or lack of clarity. In-cues and out-cues for the graphics are confirmed as well as for videos (we go to live camera in the time between prepared media). All weekend graphics including updates, song text, prayer, and liturgy are proofed, and the message content and graphics are given one last check. Sometimes we ask questions or make suggestions for changes. It's the final team huddle to verify that we have what we need. Meanwhile, down in the worship area, the band and vocalists are in full swing, rehearsing all the music to make it feel just right.

By 3:15 p.m. Mike has retreated to his office to pray and prepare, and all those involved in the worship celebration are ready for tech rehearsal. The various choirs, vocalists, band, and media team take a little break while the team leaders huddle to talk through all the nuances of the worship script, including segues, transitions, sound and lighting cues as well as stage changes. At 3:30 servants and team leaders gather on the stage for one collective prayer time, an important moment of reflection and preparation before the weekend gets under way. Once the "amen" is spoken, servants take their places. Cameras are white-balanced and focused. Microphones are checked. Lights are set, and we're off and running. We run through the music, media, spoken pieces, dramatic sketches, prayers, and whatever else needs to happen. We rehearse everything (except the message) in consecutive order and intentionally work to integrate the pieces, as I'll describe in chapter 9.

We work hard to maximize our efforts while trying to stay cool, calm, and spiritually collected. In the midst of this intense environment, we've had everything from tornado warnings to vocalist meltdowns. Stuff happens, and it's helpful to enlist support people to take care of various adjunct needs (building, maintenance, unexpected guests, and power outages) so that the worship teams can continue their preparation. Taking the time to pray has helped to ease the insanity and create the environment that will become our worship space.

By Saturday at 4:30 p.m. the worship teams are off the stage, the candles are lit, the lighting in the worship area is just right, and a carefully chosen CD is being played over the sound system. The ambience invites worshipers as the team leaders huddle in an upstairs office to talk and pray through the celebration one last time. Dinner is available for those who have been working or rehearsing all afternoon. The meal is prepared in the kitchen by servants who've discovered their gifts of service in hospitality.

At 5:00 p.m. something magical happens. The moment the band strikes the first chord of the opening music, the insanity begins to dissolve. Realizing there is no turning back, the teams move forward, opening themselves in worship. To a certain extent, whatever happens, happens. While part of the team's awareness cares very much about the people's experience and how well the celebration is going, it's impossible not to get caught up in worship. It's time to enjoy the team's creation and marvel at the ways the ordinary has intersected with the Divine–it's a miracle!

After the five o'clock celebration ends, the team takes a few deep breaths before a debriefing huddle time. The team leaders and speaker gather in a back room and ask the hard questions: How did we do? Where did we hook people? Did we distract anyone? Is the music connecting? Is the message working? Did the video inspire us? Small changes are discussed, and refinements for Sunday may be in order. Mike may distill a part of his message to make it more succinct. Confusing lines in the call to worship or the drama may need to be tweaked a little to increase the impact. It's important to do whatever it takes to lead worshipers into a powerful God experience.

Next up on the Saturday schedule is the Next Step, a worship celebration for people on the road to recovery. This alternative worship celebration, launched at Ginghamsburg in April 2005, is one of our most powerful God experiences of each week. The band is live–same as the other main campus worship gatherings–and the speaker is live as well. The rest of the Next Step team (worship hosts, greeters, ushers, testimony givers) are unpaid servants, recoverees whom God is using to assure a powerful connection for this community before, during, and after the actual worship time. Read more about the inception and progression of Next Step in chapter 11, "Alternative Worship Communities."

Sunday Serenity

By 8:00 a.m. Sunday, the rested teams are back in place. Servants have been asked to park in the spaces farthest from the building since they'll be here all morning long. Once inside, the coffee is hot, and the smiles are wide. The cameras are focusing; the projector is humming. The sound system is up, and the vocalists are in place, warming up for a long morning. Mics are rechecked and candles are relit. The tweaking is done, and now the morning's task is to take this hour-long experience and make it fresh for each incoming congregation (at 9:00, 10:15, and 11:30 a.m.). At 8:30 the team leaders huddle one last time in the war room to focus and pray together, then head to the worship area for the 9:00 a.m. worship celebration.

As the teams work their way through the morning, they gain confidence. It's great to enjoy the moments with one another, with the church family, and most of all with the God who has promised to join us if only two or more will gather in Jesus' name. The pressure of the unknown is past, and servants are doing what they love to do, whether it's pointing a camera, dialing in at the soundboard, speaking into a microphone, or playing a mean bass . . . *here we are to worship!*

WEEKLY TO-DO LIST

Speaker
- Spend time with God early in the week to determine the word and direction for the message.
- Attend the weekly worship design team meeting. Share scriptures and direction of the message with the team.
- Work on the message, seeking insight and creative assistance from an accountability group or the worship design team as needed.
- Present the finished message to the micro-team (media personnel, graphic artist, and/or creative director) so the players can create message graphics.
- Set aside time for personal refreshment to prepare and be fully present for weekend worship celebrations.
- Deliver a practice message for team players in order to view completed graphics and make necessary revisions.
- Participate in weekend worship celebrations, including adjusting the message on the spot as needed.

Team Leader (may be creative director or another person on the team)

- Prepare for and lead the weekly worship design team meeting.
- Ensure that each team player has specific, individualized direction and support before leaving the meeting.
- Think through potential needs and resources for the upcoming weekend.
- Write or oversee the writing and execution of all message-supporting worship components, including the call to worship, prayers, scriptures, stories, dramas, announcements, and closing words.
- Stay in close contact with the speaker to ensure support and cohesion with team plans.
- Attend the micro-team meeting with the speaker and other team players to create the message graphics and finalize points for the bulletin outline.
- Create a program script to clarify order of service, cues, and technical details.
- Oversee the stage design, lighting, and floor setup in the worship area.
- Set aside time for personal refreshment to prepare and be fully present for weekend worship celebrations.
- Participate in the practice message run-through session to ensure the grammatical and artistic quality of all graphics. Provide coaching or feedback to the main speaker as requested.
- Participate in all weekend worship celebrations according to areas of giftedness.

Music Director

- Obtain worship themes or scriptures in advance in order to bring song suggestions to the worship design team meeting.
- Ensure that the weekend musicians are in place.
- Attend the weekly worship design team meeting.
- Oversee the preparation and arrangement of any music needed by the band or vocalists.
- Connect with additional ministry or music teams as needed (choir, men's ensemble, women's choir, etc.) to expand the music ministry into its own community beyond the worship celebrations.
- Connect with the creative director or team leader to discuss any changes or additions to the weekend worship script (unless the music director *is* the team leader).
- Confirm worship rehearsal time and plans with all audio personnel.
- Prepare for and direct initial worship rehearsal.
- Double-check that all personnel, equipment, instruments, and support required for weekend worship are in place.
- Set aside time for personal refreshment to prepare and be fully present for weekend worship celebrations.
- Direct pre-worship music and tech rehearsal with other worship teams (drama, media, sound lighting, and so on).
- Lead entire music ministry through all of the weekend worship celebrations.

Videographer / Media Producer

- Prepare for the upcoming weekend by assuring all unpaid servants, equipment, and software supplies are secured.
- Connect with the creative director regarding upcoming themes to best prepare and generate ideas for the design team meeting.
- Attend the weekly worship design team meeting. Assist the team in researching video clips, brainstorming new media pieces, and defining a theme and look for the service.
- Secure personnel and props for video shoots as needed.
- Produce any media pieces planned for the weekend, securing help when necessary from unpaid servants or from design team players.
- Stay in contact with the graphic artist and the creative director to ensure a unified visual look for all weekend media pieces.
- Attend the micro-team meeting with the graphic artist, speaker, and creative director to create message graphics. Write cue script for agreed-upon message graphics.
- Finish production work. Double-check finished video pieces for correct sound balance and cohesion with weekend look and feel. Determine the best way to transition into and out of video pieces.
- Set aside time for personal refreshment to prepare and be fully present for weekend worship celebrations.
- Set up all technical equipment in the worship area, and work with the team to prepare all equipment and personnel for worship.
- Lead the tech rehearsal for all music, drama, and media personnel.
- Participate in the practice message run-through session to preview message graphics and video pieces along with the speaker and creative director.
- Floor-direct weekend worship celebrations if necessary.
- As time allows, train and develop new and existing media team personnel.

Graphic Artist

- Attend the weekly worship design team meeting. Give particular attention to the theme and visual elements of the message.
- Gain team input on the look of the main graphic before leaving the worship design meeting.
- Gather software, photographs, and other materials to create the main weekend worship graphic.
- Create one or two mock-ups of the main weekend graphic. Consult with other team players before finalizing this important piece.
- Attend the micro-team meeting with the other team players. Listen to the message, and create a list of graphics to be designed specifically for the message.
- Meet with the team leader/creative director to assess additional weekly worship graphic needs (for announcements, worship song lyrics, prayers, storytelling enhancements, etc.).
- Artistically create all agreed-upon weekly graphics plus additional graphics as needed (holiday, baptism, communion, special photos, etc.).
- Participate in the practice message run-through session by displaying prepared graphics as the speaker delivers the message.
- Refine or replace graphics as needed.
- Serve on the media team as needed during all weekend worship celebrations.

PART III: MAXIMIZING MULTISENSORY WORSHIP

> The courage to imagine
> the otherwise is our
> greatest resource, adding
> color and suspense to all
> our life.
> —Daniel Boorstin,
>   former Librarian of
>   Congress

Multisensory worship is worship that engages the senses. People absorb messages better when all their senses are engaged. Rather than just expect our people to listen to talking heads, we give visual representation to the message with screen graphics or video and stage displays. We invite worshipers to take the hands of the persons on either side as we go to God in prayer. Communion becomes an opportunity to "taste and see that the LORD is good" (Psalm 34:8) as we serve fresh bread dipped into the cup. Much care is given so that each worshiper feels comfortable and engaged. Jesus knew the value of a well-prepared environment. "I go and prepare a place for you," he told us (John 14:3), and then promised he'd come back to take us there one day soon.

In this section you'll find practical steps and valuable insights to help you incorporate multisensory elements into your worship celebrations. We'll start up front on the platform, then work our way back through the entire worship area. Get ready for some moving and shaking—your worship spaces may never look quite the same again!

CHAPTER 7
THE MAGIC OF MUSIC AND MEDIA

*The best and most beautiful things in
the world cannot be seen nor even touched,
but just felt in the heart.*
—Helen Keller

Each week as the Ginghamsburg team players meet to design worship together, someone will inevitably pipe up and ask, "What is the *vibe* we're going for here this week?"

It's an excellent question. I love that question. It's proof positive that designing powerful God experiences goes way beyond the cerebral to something much deeper inside us. It's a question that invites the team to begin describing the worship celebration to one another in terms like *edgy*, *high-feel*, *ancient-future*, *urban*, or *earthy*, just to name a few. (The words get made up as we go along!) It's a well-known fact that God is not limited to any particular vibe. God can work through all of them.

The team's agreement on the vibe gives the stage designer more input on how to style the stage. The videographer can better decide how to stylize the videos. The graphic designer sees a clearer picture of how to best design the graphics, and the musical worship leader can go to work researching the absolute best songs for the most effective worship experience. The entire team is ever aware that the ultimate purpose of any media or music piece will be to put the speaker on the five-yard line of the worship field, so to speak, so that (worst-case scenario) all the speaker has to do is to fall over the goal line and score!

MUSIC THAT CATCHES THE HEART OF GOD

He taught me how to sing the latest God-song,
*   a praise-song to our God.*
More and more people are seeing this:
*   they enter the mystery,*
*   abandoning themselves to GOD.*
*   —Psalm 40:3 The Message*

Music is a powerful form of connection and communication as it plays to both sides of the brain at the same time. The tones keep the right side busy so that the messages can be absorbed into the left. Our team works hard to identify the musical styles that will enable the maximum number of people to connect to the celebration, to the message, and ultimately, to Jesus.

How is it possible to find music that will pour God's love into the hearts of worshipers needing a divine touch? And conversely, how can we create atmospheres of worship where our congregations passionately communicate the depth of their love to God?

Throughout the years, Ginghamsburg has developed a worship music style that transcends the individual leaders, players, and vocalists. That style has been consistently characterized by three key components: diversity, passion, and challenge.

Diversity is easily understood, less easily demonstrated. Something we've done fairly well is to feature many styles of music within the same celebration, sometimes within the same song. For instance, rather than bemoan the fact that not everyone loves classic rock, we simply give the hymn lovers a taste of their own dessert. Guns N' Roses segues into "Amazing Grace." "Can't Give Up Now" (Mary Mary) meanders into Coldplay. The true picture of the kingdom of God boasts a wide array of colors, tastes, and radio stations—and that's a good thing!

I once asked Francis Wyatt, who was Ginghamsburg's music director at the time, to share what he most looked for in a musician.

"Passion!" He quickly said, "First and foremost is passion. It's not so much about being technically proficient; however, I do truly appreciate that. But I've heard many technically advanced musicians whose passion stops for no apparent reason when they pick up the instrument. I've heard musicians who've had limited proficiency of the instrument, and yet are somehow able to communicate exactly how they feel at that moment with passion. So for me, the first thing I look for in musicians is passion. Once they have passion, you can teach them everything else. You can teach them how to play better, faster, and with more advanced harmonies, but it is very hard to teach passion." Truly, the musicians' demonstration of passion invites the worshipers to feel their own emotion and empowers the songs to soar.

Passion helps fuel the challenge factor. All of us need to be challenged to grow past our comfort zones. Each time we gather to worship, our expectation is that this experience will challenge and change us, and music is the single greatest catalyst to prepare for that change. Great music challenges us to move closer to God. It moves us to embrace one another's ethnicity. Worshipful music calls us to stand up and be counted among God's faithful servants; to live out our missional call. We all need to be challenged toward growth, and music powerfully calls us to respond.

Paul Jones has been the director of music at Ginghamsburg Church long enough to be able to describe some of the uniqueness of how the Ginghamsburg worship team dreams and plans together. Here's what Paul had to say:

> People cannot believe that our design team sits down with our pastor on Wednesdays to plan for the upcoming weekend. We like to think of it as the Holy Spirit working in real time with us—in the design team moments and conversation. Many worship leaders seem to have to plan worship in a vacuum, but because of our pastor's participation with us, we are able to crawl into his or her message and be there with our song choices. We're choosing music that will speak to the people's hearts and enhance that specific message. We're able to move in one unified direction and complement the message effectively.
>
> If the message is heavy, for instance, we might plan some healing songs at the top of the celebration to prepare people's hearts. If it's a student-led weekend, we want the vibe of the music to reflect the culture of the students. These kinds of experiences stretch our congregation into new styles and deepen our sense of community as well.

When researching songs to enhance message themes, I typically go to iTunes top 100 songs, Billboard Music, CCLI's Song Select, Worship Leader Magazine's Song Discovery, and Pandora Radio, which creates playlists based on information you type in. In addition, while hearing Mike's rough early version of the message we'll quickly e-mail a larger "team" of musical thinkers (servants we've come to know from our ministry) with the message theme and ask their thoughts and ideas for weekend music choices. Often they will e-mail right back with suggestions, widening the cultural choices and tastes that we choose from week to week.

The trick for us is finding the songs that speak to the people, are relevant to the message, and can be effectively delivered by the scheduled musicians for any given weekend. When all these forces line up and the songs really work, that's my God moment. When these pieces don't line up, well, that makes it work rather than worship . . . ouch!

Leading the music teams is a calling I share with others as we serve the larger congregation together, week after week after week. I realize each moment that I'm part of a much larger team, and my role is to make sure we really bring it.

And bring it they will. I love the music at Ginghamsburg, the way it's stretching us and growing us into a multicultural community. I am drawn into worship from the moment the first chord is struck until the final notes of the celebration.

It's our prayer that our songs—the *new* songs we sing—will soar beyond the walls and rafters of our earthly worship spaces and reach right up to heaven . . . music that catches the heart of God.

MEDIA: FOCUSING ON TRANSFORMATION

Make visible what, without you, might perhaps never have been seen.
—Robert Bresson

Dreaming and teaming up to provide effective media pieces for worship celebrations have been natural parts of our weekly process. Every media producer and graphic artist who's been part of our team's evolution has added his or her unique skill and visual theology to the style we currently embrace. Other worship team players who are not formally trained in media production frequently contribute ideas and thoughts as well. Although not media experts by any stretch of the imagination, we're all life-livers. We dabble in media design because it affords us the opportunity to bring more human life, more people stories, more of God's creation, more culture, and more candor into our worship experiences.

Visual storytelling invites us into life scenarios we may not have previously experienced for ourselves. Without media, it's easy for people to begin to think, *Life is all about me.* Yet when I see a homeless person on the screen as I hear U2's "Beautiful Day," I am reminded that "there but for the grace of God go I." When I see the story of a mom who lost her teenage daughter to a train collision, I am reminded to be thankful for and enjoy present moments with my daughter, who is alive. Media invite us into the lives and experiences of other people. Effective media touch our hearts and minds at a very deep level and move us to laughter and prayers, to tears and transformation.

In my early years of worship design I was coerced into a grand, albeit spur-of-the-moment skydiving experience to use as an illustrative metaphor in our worship celebrations for the upcoming weekend. We were able to capture the entire experience on video, and when we shared that piece in the weekend celebrations, I virtually took three thousand people up ten thousand feet into the air with me, and then we jumped out of a plane—together. We experienced the Green County, Ohio, landscape; the rush of the chute opening up; the relief of the soft landing—together. Media pieces at their best bring the outside world into our worship spaces. We experience it, connect it to God's message, and then take that message out into our world and lives.

TELLING OUR STORIES

Todd Carter served as chief videographer on the Ginghamsburg team for a number of years. His deep understanding of powerful media afforded us the invaluable gift of his daily work, helping to form our current media-intensive worship culture. Todd is a media soldier; he was up early in the morning and late into the night when the project demanded it. His call is to discover the people-story inside each assignment, and he doesn't let up until his perspiration evokes the congregation's inspiration. Here's Todd's description of the power of storytelling through media ministry:

> *Media ministry calls us to make local heroes out of the people in our congregations by telling their stories. Stories can be told in many different ways; and most effective stories have a "hook," some aspect that makes you think, Okay, I can see myself in that. That kind of story is relevant.*
>
> *I like doing stories that focus on real-life, everyday people that are just doing the best that they can in their Jesus journey. We communicate where they were before, where they are today, what happened (the hook), and where they see themselves going. It's similar to the old testimony format.*
>
> *A well-told story is not unlike a well-written paper where you take lots of different bits and pieces of information and put them together in a visually cohesive way. It's like a puzzle where the pieces all fit together to make a whole. When that happens, it's magic. If a story touches not only your head but also your heart, chances are that you are just getting out of the way and letting God do the work as the story tells itself.*
>
> *Leave the doors open to new, creative ideas that have never been done—sometimes they'll work and sometimes they won't. If you're not willing to try, however, you'll never go beyond where you are right now. Technology is not the devil—although it does seem to be possessed at times! Even if you don't understand it or have time to learn it, find someone in the church who does; then turn that person loose to see what he or she can come up with. I believe we are only beginning to see what could prove to be a creative revolution in our faith communities. It's a great time to be in the church.*

We live in a media-saturated world. Rather than try to escape or pretend it isn't so, we must harness the power of media for God's best purposes. Through digital storytelling, graphic imagery, worshipful artistry, mission moments, and myriad other possibilities, we can elevate this earthly form to an eternal function. And as we do so, God will be honored.

CHAPTER 8
STYLING THE STAGE

Think left and think right and think low and think high. Oh, the THINKS you can think up if only you try!
—Dr. Seuss, Oh, the Thinks You Can Think!

I come from a long line of furniture rearrangers. My earliest memories are of my mom and her mom sitting in my grandmother's living room (actually a remodeled one-room schoolhouse) talking through all the possibilities a furnished room could offer. They were always mentally arranging and rearranging things, then they would share their ideas with each other.

"We could put the piano on that south wall, Marian."

"But where would we put Great-grandma's hutch?"

"Well, it could move around to the wall over next to the window. The light would still flow in real nice."

"I never thought of that! Still, the old secretary would need to go. It's been crowded ever since you brought that old thing out here."

"You're right. I'll get Daddy to move it back to the bedroom."

On and on they went. It was like therapy for Depression-weary minds. I'd listen intently and try to picture each move they described right along with them. What that gentle banter taught me early on was that things can be rearranged. They can change. Despite our limited financial resources, we're not stuck here with the "same ol', same ol'." We can make the very same room look totally different every single week if we want to. As my colleague Sue Nilson Kibbey announces upon her arrival at the office each morning, "All-new day, all-new chances!" I truly love the concept that we can change our environment to suit the needs of the occasion.

Imagine my dismay when I first stepped inside a traditional church building and found all the furniture in the sanctuary bolted to the floor! That particular church configuration spoke volumes to my spirit. It said, "We're committed to never changing; we must keep things exactly as they are week after week, year after year." Thankfully, worshiping communities inhabiting even the most traditionally furnished church buildings are discovering new ways to use old spaces. Whether it's removing some fixtures from the platform, placing media screens in tasteful locations, or adding candles or other sources of warm, ambient light, there is always a way to breathe new life into the worship space.

Postmodern worship is best expressed in pictures and stories in the authentic context of where real people live. Styling the stage is simply creating a fresh environment where the story, message, and theme of the weekend can be best expressed and lived out.

At Ginghamsburg, we accomplish this through a team effort that includes brainstorming together, drawing in all the factors we can, and continuing to think and dream together as we begin physically creating the environment. Allow me to take you through the various steps of this informal and artistic process.

THE PREPARATION

We are working with a guest speaker this weekend, a delightful young Hispanic woman who, though ordained in her native Mexico, serves an Ohio pastorate close by. Early on I began thinking about how we might take full advantage of this speaker's ethnic perspective, and I encouraged the team to pull out their most creative Latin- or Mexican-related pieces. In the hallway and lobby areas, we will serve salsa and chips arranged on tables featuring chili peppers as décor. In the worship area we'll hear the sounds of Salvador (an excellent Latin American band) prior to each worship celebration. On the large screen will be a main graphic created to give visual image to Lupina's message. Here are the elements of the message that Lupina will bring to us:

Word: 1 John 4:16-21

Felt need: My life's pain keeps me from receiving and giving authentic love.

Desired outcome: Participants will receive and begin speaking God's language of love.

Theme: Love—The Universal Language

Look: A multicolored (red, green, yellow, orange) globe with the word *love* written on it in multiple languages

The team labored over this graphic together, giving the colors and feel a lot of tweaking and reworking until everyone felt it made just the right statement, painted just the right picture. Since we associate Mexico with bright colors, we've opted to bring out the reds, greens, yellows, and oranges—all gel colors we've inserted into the lighting cans that will throw warm light onto the back walls of the stage area. This careful attention to the lighting to pull out the main graphic colors on the screen literally transforms the environment of the large room. Its bright, warming presence invites worshipers to come in and take part. "Something good is going to happen in here," the atmosphere whispers, and our prayer is that our people will experience a culturally rich worship encounter.

For the stage décor, Lupina will bring maracas and some personal items from her homeland for us to draw from. Another Ginghamsburg family has been to Mexico on mission numerous times, and we've asked for blankets, clothing, or other themed items. It's unusual for me not to know *exactly* what we'll end up with until Saturday, so I am feeling a bit anxious. But I'm trusting that we'll be able to pull it together with God's help. With the key colors in mind, we've already set aside red, orange, and yellow candles from our candle stash to use on candle stands of varying heights.

As I've mentally designed the stage, I know this celebration will have at least two great elements. I anticipate that the music, planned with a Latin feel, will be nothing short of exciting. Early in the planning stages we scheduled extra horns to help the songs be fun and worshipful (yes, fun and worshipful can coexist!). I'm also excited about our video in production, a retelling of our recent adult mission trip to Mexico. Because our team connects throughout the week, the finished video will include the colors, music bed, and feel of our other worship elements. This combination of our best work represents *my* best translation of Romans 8:28: "And we know that in all things [design elements, media, artistic creations, music selections] God works for the good for those who *love him*, who have been called according to *his purpose*!"

THE RESULTING EXPERIENCE

In the end, our Hispanic weekend was all we had hoped it would be. Some people brought their chips and salsa into the worship area. It was a fun event. The Latin-style music came alive. The video featured our bright color scheme and a music bed with a Mexican feel. Our digital story captured the adult mission team excitedly describing the home they had built from the ground up for a mother of six in Tijuana, Mexico.

The stage displays included woven blankets, baskets, the colored candles, and Lupina's various artifacts, including her Spanish Bible. We placed a large piece of framed artwork (supplied by Lupina) on an easel flanked by candle stands at the main entrance to the worship area. Extending the worship-themed décor to the entryways, the lobby, and even the outside walkways, when possible, builds anticipation for an exciting and meaningful worship experience.

Lupina's message was powerful as, with a distinct Hispanic accent, she boldly described God's inclusive heart of love. Looking back, we did not simply hear a message from a Hispanic pastor. To be in the worship celebration that day was to *feel* the heartbeat of the Mexican people as we allowed ourselves to consider our part in learning God's language of love. All in all, it was a powerful cross-cultural, multisensory God experience.

Multisensory worship is a given at Ginghamsburg. It never fails to move us. But will it move you? Do you dare to try it in your church?

Right now I'm pretty sure I hear someone saying, "Isn't God enough? Why do we need all this stuff to create environment?" (Trust me. Some weeks I've been tempted to ask that!) The truth is that while God may be temporarily invisible to us, God's creation is all around us—and it reflects the glory of God.

God has gifted us with an unending palette of color and an incredible montage of humanity. In these elements we catch glimpses of God's character. We only have to turn and look around our world to be reminded that our God is a God of amazing variety. Why not celebrate that variety in worship?

All of creation sings the glory of God. Each weekend we attempt to portray one small part of God's character. As human beings made in God's image, we use God's palette of color to brighten dark lives. We imitate God's creative initiative toward humankind as we present the gospel using metaphors, parables, and real-life stories. In this we follow the example of Jesus, who often spoke in metaphors and frequently used visual imagery to describe timeless truth. "I will make you *fishers* of men," Jesus said (Matthew 4:19, emphasis added). "You are the *salt* of the earth" (Matthew 5:13, emphasis added). Styling the stage is our effort to bring God's imagery to life, to provide for ourselves a place inside the story, to be in the moment with God.

CREATING SPACES

As you begin to re-create your worship space, identify several places to arrange key anchor displays. It is impossible and unnecessary to redecorate an entire worship area. Most of the time I've found it best to focus on two or three key locations where visual displays would enhance the message. Not sure where to start? Try the stage, perhaps in an area originally created for an altar-type arrangement. These displays are like modern-day altars, places where we can meet God and be reminded of God's presence and power.

In our environment we often create two anchor displays, one on either end of the large stage, and sometimes a smaller version closer to the center. Doing this allows more people in the room to see and experience the display. Overall balance is important, so we look at the different pieces we'll have on the stage each weekend and allow what is happening with people to dictate décor placement. The band is usually fairly stationary, but other people or props may require space in the stage area. Additional musicians, interview sets, a drama or a dance, a table with communion elements, or even stacks of the Bibles we give out to third graders once a year require dedicated space. Each weekend's unique segments require us to constantly rethink our placement, always creating a fresh picture of worship. I love this challenge—"all-new day, all-new chances!" It's like getting a new worship space every single weekend, fifty-two times a year.

Sometimes our rearrangements become semipermanent. (Nothing is ever truly permanent here, except the truth of the message!) One weekend we needed to change our balcony space. The balcony was a flat area where rows of minimally engaged participants had been expected to watch a TV monitor for their worship experience. We wanted to provide a more community-friendly environment, a café-type atmosphere. To create the change, we purchased every black metal patio table we could find in the entire Dayton area. We spread the tables throughout the balcony, lit a votive candle in the center of each one, and set our nicest chairs around them. We added a couple of strategically placed monitors and made soft drinks available for a minimal donation. The re-created worship seating is now much more hospitable than the rows of chairs had been.

Encouraged by our success in the balcony, we kept going. When our Saturday evening worship attendance numbers allow, we take out the last few rows of chairs in the main worship area and add twelve large, round tables across the back. We place chairs around these tables so they face the front of the room. Seating space does not permit us to do this on Sunday mornings, but our Saturday evening crowd loves this more casual table seating. Worshipers grab these tables right away and enjoy the opportunity to gather and worship with a small group of friends. Discover more new ideas for worship seating and spaces in chapter 11, "Alternative Worship Communities," or visit the Redesigning Worship blog at www.redesigningworship.blogspot.com.

Great things can happen when you dare to change. As you work to create new environments, however, always keep in mind the needs of your team members. In our experience, we've noticed that onstage team members such as speakers, drama players, or musicians can become a little anxious about their space. They usually have a good idea of what kind of space (and how much space) they need to accomplish their roles in the celebration. If physical environment changes are in the works, it's best to talk over any special challenges ahead of time to avoid last-minute trauma. We try to promote an atmosphere of flexibility, and we encourage ourselves not to become too territorial. Being able to strategize together ahead of time seems to be the key. But even that hasn't totally eliminated what I refer to as . . .

DRAMA TRAUMA

Most worship areas have their unique challenges, and ours is no exception. We have no real dedicated drama space, so we've tried to think of the entire room as the actors' potential arena. We've used aisles, balcony space, center stage, and stage left—what we refer to as our "drama wing." (It sounds a lot more glamorous than it is.) Unfortunately, any drama set or furniture we might want to leave there permanently would prevent members of our Deaf community from seeing the screen and prevent the audience from seeing the vocal ensemble. We keep working on new drama placement ideas, but for now this situation provides a good reminder that we *all* have challenges to overcome and less than ideal circumstances to think through.

One Christmas Eve we staged two modern-day angels delivering monologues from two upper-ledge storage areas looking out over the audience—complete with fog-machine enhancement! Once a very disturbed man came into a worship gathering and climbed onto the stage to verbally attack the speaker. Several worshipers later told us that they thought it was part of the drama! Since we have so many unique dramatic sets and scenarios, we've since promised to let our security team know when someone from the floor is *supposed* to come onto the stage.

BEAUTY AND THE BUDGET: SUPPLIES FOR YOUR CREATIVE CLOSET

In order to produce dramas and style stages, you'll need props. Where are you going to get them? More important once you find out where to get them, how are you going to pay for them? Although the physical enhancements I've described may seem costly, we've actually spent very little to obtain them. We're constantly asking ourselves, "What is already here that we can use for this purpose? What do we have that can find new life in a stage display?"

We use a few standard pieces (mostly homemade) again and again to support the stage look each week. These pieces provide a framework or backdrop for any specific thematic pieces we might want to add. Here's a list of some basic pieces from our closet of possibilities. The list describes the pieces we've found most helpful and how we made or acquired them.

Black Boxes

Years ago I realized that we were going to need some way to create displays on the stage. I started paying attention to the displays in department stores and came upon the idea of the black box. It is painted glossy black on five sides, with one end open. A Ginghamsburg servant made ours from half-inch plywood. We now have six large boxes (twenty-four-by-eighteen-by-eighteen inches) and two small ones (eighteen-by-twelve-by-twelve inches). We can turn them, stack them, and use them alone or place next to each other. They have been stools for reader's theater and individual stands for communion elements. They also make handy table stands for extra musical equipment. They always look great on stage without distracting from the professional look. Black boxes (made of plastic) are available from catalogs, but we made our own very economically and in just the sizes we needed. We repaint them every so often to keep them looking nice.

Old Wooden Crates

These serve as another alternative for our box-type needs. We acquired a large collection from a landscape nursery for next to nothing. These aged crates create a more natural, organic look. While we can use them the same way as the black boxes, their distinct look communicates an entirely different vibe. Choices are good!

Antique Communion Table

Although we used a large fancy communion table at one time, it always felt like church hardware to me. It was extremely formal looking (we're not very formal) and took up an enormous amount of valuable floor space needed for people. We now use that larger table only for weddings. In its place, we purchased a smaller, simpler table from an antique store. The tabletop is wood, matching the crates. We painted the legs black to match the stage skirting and the black boxes. Since we have the freedom to move things around, we find endless ways to use this piece of stage furniture.

Old Rugged Cross

We don't have a cross hanging on the wall in our worship area, but we do have the option to use a cross as often as we want to. Our "old rugged cross" is six-by-ten feet and probably made from old four-by-fours. Because scripture never specifies that the cross of Jesus was both upright and empty at the same time, I tried not to worry too much when the stand for this wooden cross suddenly disappeared one week. I began laying the cross on its side at an angle on the stage, propping it against black boxes or crates with cement blocks inside for stability.

We've put the cross in a number of different places on the stage and arranged candles, draped cloth, or added other supporting visual pieces around it. On communion weekends (the first weekend of each month) we frequently set broken bread and a goblet in front of the cross on a small box. These different arrangements cause us to consider the meaning of the cross in new ways, inviting greater appreciation for all that Jesus has done for us.

Urban Cross

A few years ago on one weekend we needed a different kind of cross—one of less natural wood providing more of an urban feel to connect with our brothers and sisters in the city. We purchased metal signpost material and created a five-by-seven-foot cross. After painting it black, a Ginghamsburg servant created a stand by welding this cross to a large circular metal base. Now we have the choice of two totally different crosses to enhance two looks, depending on the overall feel of the weekend.

LIGHTING

Candles

There are several things to keep in mind about candles. The first is safety. Always check ahead of time for potentially dangerous situations when you use candles. As much as possible, set candles away from the general flow of people traffic. If people are concerned about open flames, place clear glass hurricane covers over lit candles. We've always been able to work within these guidelines, and in a dozen years of creating multisensory worship settings, we have never had a fire. (We've had some humorous situations, but that's another book!) So far we've managed to provide safe spaces for ministry without losing a creative edge.

Candles are truly effective pieces of the overall multisensory experience. However, using them week after week can be costly. We've developed a few ways to keep the cost down and the effectiveness up:

- Watch for great sales. As with everything you buy, make this your motto: *never* pay full price!
- Choose three-inch-wide candles (sometimes called chunky). Cared for well, they burn a long, long time. In contrast, tapers are fast burners in a room where air vent fans are blowing (our challenge), and fast-burning candles make a mess.
- Consider the color. Flames burning inside large dark-colored candles cannot be seen from a distance, lessening their effectiveness for use on stage. Lighter colors such as whites and yellows cause the flame inside the candle to appear as a dancing glow, which maximizes its effectiveness.
- Select very hard, more expensive candles. They will last longer than softer ones and may be the best choice if you can find them on sale.
- Trim longer wicks to about one-half inch. Doing this each time the candles are lit will keep the candles from producing smoky flames. Some candles may need the wax to be poured out from time to time.
- Place a sheet of fabric, paper, plastic, or Plexiglas under the candle stands to prevent wax from spilling onto the carpet. If wax does drip onto fabric or carpet, you can repair the damage by (1) scraping the excess wax off the surface, (2) placing paper towels over the spot and ironing with a hot iron (the paper towels will blot up the wax), and (3) writing a note of apology to the custodian or housekeeping personnel!

Candle Stands

Candle stands have become an absolute must for creating any sort of intimate worship gathering. Usually found in sets of varying heights, they can be used again and again. On communion weekends, they highlight the cross. Some weeks we space them evenly across the front of the stage; other weeks they create a backdrop for a vocal ensemble. Candle stands elevate lit candles so they can be seen from quite a distance. Even worshipers just entering the room can see the lit candles and immediately feel welcomed.

Inquiring minds usually want to know where to find candle stands at modest prices. Depending on your geographic location, I suggest Pier 1 Imports (wait for a sale!), Value City, Sam's Club, Costco, and Hobby Lobby. Various websites and boutiques can be helpful as well. (My motto is to always be on the lookout for cool, high-quality but inexpensive stage stuff!) Buying several sets of candle stands allows for flexible and portable display options, and the initial investment will provide long-term benefit. Candle stands can also be used by others in the church for weddings and funerals, and should be stored in or near . . .

A Dedicated Candle Closet

Storing sets of colored candles together in a closet or large cupboard is helpful and will encourage others in your church to use candles for their events. Labeled shelves enable different ministry groups to use the candles, then return them to their proper places (so you can find them when you need them). We always hope other teams will take advantage of our candle closet because at Ginghamsburg we don't encourage only multisensory worship; we also encourage multisensory ministry!

Pin Lights

These small "can" lights are available through commercial lighting catalogs. Some more industrial-looking stage displays are effectively enhanced with spotlighting rather than candles. We keep on hand six pin spots that we can plug in on location to throw a small ray of focused light onto key areas. Colored gel paper can be inserted into the pin lights to change their effect.

Lanterns

Lanterns are a great décor possibility and are often available through craft stores, Odd Lots, or Pottery Barn. Hanging them at varying heights creates a great ambience, but for a while we didn't know how to accomplish this, which brings me to the last item in our creative closet . . .

Large Shepherd Hook Lantern Stands

One Christmas we wanted to hang nine lanterns (we'd found them at Odd Lots), and we needed a cost-effective way to do that. A talented Ginghamsburg servant created hanger stands by welding them out of rebar, the textured metal rod found in poured cement. (You can purchase rebar at a lumber store or other building materials store.)

Our creator of the hangers shaped the rebar into a shepherd's hook at the top, with a small *v* turned on the very end to accommodate the lantern handle. To make the hooks free-standing, he added a three-pronged base at the bottom, formed by welding together three twelve-inch pieces of rebar. We now have three sets of differing heights. Although the hangers were originally intended for the lantern service, we use them to hang signs, drape fabric, or suspend strings of lights. Maybe additional uses have come to mind as you've been reading!

Sometimes these standard pieces from our closet are all it takes to create the environment for our worship celebrations. Sometimes we add a few others. By mixing and matching these items in different ways, we create a vast array of worship environments. Creating beauty on a budget is entirely possible!

ACQUIRING THE UNUSUAL WITHOUT OPENING THE WALLET

As we dream big worship dreams, we sit around the table and visualize the resulting worship celebration. And then we have to stop and ask ourselves, "Wait a minute—how on earth are we going to make *that* happen? How are we going to persuade the amusement park to allow our videographer and his equipment inside? How are we going to get those motorcycles parked on the stage? How is this forty-something mother of three going to get up the courage to show up at a skydiving appointment and jump out of an airplane?" (That was me, remember!) All with God's help, that's how.

Over time we've really come to trust that with God's help, it *will* happen; oh, yes, it will. To allow ourselves the escape route of "maybe it's just not God's will" provides an easy way out. We don't dare think that might be true until five o'clock on Saturday when the first weekend celebration begins. Until then, we keep trying. Many weeks we've had to really rack our brains to figure it all out, but when God helps us succeed, the rewards are great.

I can recall a weekend when we wanted to tell the story of the woman at the well. We had a great script adapted from John 4. We had a storyteller, but alas, no well. "Where to find a well?" we wondered. Finding one seemed an expensive and impossible goal, since none of us had a clue about where to look. "Let's make our own," our summer worship intern suggested. And we went for it!

We gathered about thirty cement blocks and formed them into a four-foot-wide circle, three layers high. We found rounded red decorative bricks in the Ginghamsburg garage to place into the wedge-shaped cracks between the blocks. We got a really thick rope out of my garage, threw one end into the "well," and wrapped the other end around the handle of an old wooden bucket. *Voilà*, a well! We had a place for our storyteller to inhabit while telling about Jesus' encounter with the Samaritan woman.

Water always inspires us to do great things. One weekend Mike chose to talk about our Living Water, available as a continuous source of refreshment (John 4:10-14). We called the celebration "Thirsty." We thought about using water in the environment. We *dreamed* about using running water. I had seen a shop in Tipp City that sold small decorative fountains with running water. I knew we could never afford those fountains at a cost of more than a hundred dollars each. So I asked the store's owner if we could borrow them for our worship display. She said that we could, and she and I brainstormed together how our stage team might pick them up and return them to the shop without her losing valuable sales time. (I like creating win-win partnerships.)

Every corner of the worship area that weekend was multisensory. We set up fountains in the entryway and on the stage. Between celebrations, we played a CD with sounds of flowing water and a moving water animation video on the screen. (Did a lot of people leave worship to use the restroom, or did I just imagine that?) We acquired the unusual without opening the wallet.

One weekend Mike wanted to preach about our need for the full armor of God, but he wanted to update it somehow. This idea presented just the kind of challenge our team loves. "How about an 'Armor of God' fashion show?" someone suggested. "We could feature each piece on individual models." The team agreed on the direction, and we called it "Dressed for Success." We used these elements:

Word: Ephesians 6:10-17

Felt need: I'm too vulnerable in my humanity to be successful.

Desired outcome: Participants will get dressed (with the full armor of God)!

Theme: Dressed for Success

Look: Runway and a glitzy fashion show with models wearing armor pieces

Wednesday afternoon we began searching for armor by calling Christian supply stores. Finally, at a party costume shop we found a plastic breastplate, shield, belt, and helmet. All of these armor accessories were metallic gold and silver. So we spray painted an old pair of boots gold and borrowed a samurai sword—armor complete. (These pieces weren't all free, granted, but the cost was still fairly minimal.)

Mike had been careful in Wednesday's team meeting to explain the usefulness of each piece of armor. We developed a character for each armor item. I wrote a "Call to Wardrobe" drama script. On Friday, a team reconfigured the stage to create a runway that went into the congregation. (Our staging pieces are like LEGO building blocks—you can build whatever you imagine.) The band introduced the drama with the ZZ Top song "Sharp Dressed Man." We'd made a little behind-the-scenes video to set it up, featuring the models arguing in the makeshift dressing room. One of our vocalists narrated in her best French accent. Everyone really got into it, and once we'd edged the stage and runway with little white minilights (look in your Christmas closet!), it definitely did not look like a typical worship area. Truthfully, I had a tiny fear that we had really gone over the top.

In the end, much to our surprise, *everyone* loved it. Older folks loved it; young people loved it. (You'll find the script in the appendix.) I believe the reason we didn't receive even one complaint about going over the top was that the spiritual message—our desperate human need for God's armor in the battle of life—was so powerful that it felt like God's hand was all over that celebration. It's the only way to explain it. It felt great that all of us (the drama players, the singers, the band, the lighting and the camera teams) were able to use our gifts in such an out-of-the-box way. The congregation was edified, realizing the kind of God-clothing we all have available, and God was truly honored in our discovery.

Okay, so we *are* a little crazy and we *do* go to extremes once in a while, but after all is said and done, worship is something we can and should give our lives to. This is the most awesome community to work among, because we have the greatest story to tell. It's invigorating to know that we've created something together that will influence lives for years to come. We've dreamed the unusual to accomplish the impossible, and each of us believes that "I can do everything through him who gives me strength" (Philippians 4:13).

ASK, SEEK, KNOCK

We could have said no when we couldn't figure out where to get a well, how to find the armor, or where to go for running water. When no is not an option, we'll all work a lot harder to make things happen—and we'll be helped by the One who has promised to do *exceedingly and abundantly* more than all we ask or think!

Now to him who is able to do immeasurably more than all we ask or imagine, according to his power that is at work within us, to him be glory in the church and in Christ Jesus throughout all generations, for ever and ever!
—Ephesians 3:20-21

When you encounter challenges in worship planning, discouragement can easily set in. We all get discouraged, but we don't have to stay discouraged. Staying discouraged wastes valuable time. Keep asking, keep seeking, and keep working toward the goal: powerful God experiences!

CHAPTER 9
WRITING FOR WORSHIP CONNECTION

I am a little pencil in the hand of
a writing God who is sending a
love letter to the world
—Mother Teresa

It's 11:31 p.m. and time for David Letterman. I'm a news junkie, and I've just finished watching the eleven o'clock news when I see the camera pan over the Hudson River and across the New York City skyline. *Late Show with David Letterman* appears in that familiar font, and I hear the announcer introduce the show in that familiar voice. Not three seconds pass before I hear the hook—the names of the guests to be on the show that night. It is in those first ten seconds that I decide, *Should I stay or should I go? Should I watch Dave, switch over to Conan, or just give it up and go to sleep?*

It's 10:33 Sunday morning. Monty Postmodern is sitting close to the center aisle, halfway back in the worship area. The opening music has just concluded, and a worship host walks to the center stage, picks up the microphone, and begins to speak. It's in those first ten seconds that Monty will decide whether he should stay or go.

At least that's how I try to think about it. That's the kind of importance I assign to the work of writing the connection pieces for worship celebrations. And while Monty and any of his postmodern pew-partners may not physically get up and leave the worship area, in the remote control of his mind he has full ability to press the channel button up or down and think about breakfast, lunch, golf, or tomorrow's presentation at the office.

The mind, however, is a terrible thing to waste. And if Monty has gone to the trouble of getting dressed for church, piling his children into the car, and finding a parking space, I want to make sure that we've done all we can to make his efforts worthwhile. My mission is to connect people to Jesus in creative ways, and I figure we're not going to get a second chance to make a powerful first impression.

REACH OUT AND TOUCH

Crafting connection pieces for worship celebrations presents a significant opportunity to verbally reach out and touch others. Whether we are writing a call to worship, a prayer of confession, an interview, a drama, communion words, or announcements, what we say and how we say it will make all the difference in the world as we design powerful worship experiences. If God is "not wanting anyone to perish, but everyone to come to repentance" (2 Peter 3:9b), then we must passionately partner with God to "take captive every thought to make it obedient to Christ."

The weapons we fight with are not weapons of the world. On the contrary, they have divine power to demolish strongholds. We demolish arguments and every pretension that sets itself up against the knowledge of God, and we take captive every thought to make it obedient to Christ.
—2 Corinthians 10:4-5

As writers and communicators, we have the task of focusing people's minds and hearts on what God truly wants to say to them. That is why even these connecting pieces must always be message centered and thoughtfully prepared.

If then I do not grasp the meaning of what someone is saying, I am a foreigner to the speaker, and he is a foreigner to me.
—1 Corinthians 14:11

When I put together my thoughts for a call to worship, I think about the big picture of the worship celebration and where we want to go, then ask how we might best grab our people's attention. Here are the elements I try to include:

- the felt need (a hook, question, statement)
- the desired outcome of the celebration
- the word or a small portion of it
- the theme with its coordinating graphic
- a segue into the song celebration or other next segment

For example, one August weekend we wanted to lift up our student ministry team and its vision to our congregation. Mike wanted to talk about our responsibility as parents, pastors, and providers to make sure our kids have every opportunity to journey with Jesus. The theme was "Road Rules." We opened the celebration with "Teach Your Children" (Crosby, Stills, Nash and Young), and then the worship host said these words as our call to worship:

> If life is a journey, then there's got to be some rules of the road. Rules that keep us on track with the One who called himself the way, the truth, and the life. The greatest trust that you and I have is to pass these road rules on to our children.
>
> Listen to how God calls us in Deuteronomy, chapter 11 (slightly paraphrased): "Teach your children well. Fix my words on your hearts and minds, and then talk about them when you sit at home and when you walk along the road together, when you lie down and when you get up. Write them wherever they will be seen, so that you and your children may be blessed," . . . because ultimately, we all want to live life just like Jesus.

The carefully chosen words of this call to worship began by introducing the theme and ended by introducing our first worship song, an original Ginghamsburg favorite at the time, "Just Like You." In place of a traditional call to worship, you can start off with a drama or a story that introduces the felt need, followed by a simple transition into a prayer or song. (For more examples of creative ways to open a celebration, check out Kim Miller's *Handbook for Multisensory Worship*, volumes 1 and 2 [Nashville: Abingdon Press, 1999, 2001].)

No matter what words we use, it's important to keep making sense and keep connecting the dots. Even announcements will take on new meaning when they are connected to the overall message. Anything that occurs during congregational time should pertain to everyone in some way, as well as connect to the overall mission of the church. Here's an example: "Next weekend's Community Festival is our biggest outreach opportunity of the year as we seek to 'bring seeking people into a life-Celebration of Jesus,' which is the first part of Ginghamsburg's mission statement. We want to get the word out to friends, neighbors, and coworkers about this exciting event!" Information that applies only to certain groups is better shared in writing or on a church website if you have one.

When members of a congregation are moving forward in mission together, the announcements are action steps toward the mission. We use announcements as part of our constant, strategic, and intentional communication about where we're going as a movement. When we connect these messages to the mission, we witness a surge in its momentum.

LESS IS MORE

If I've heard Mike say this once, I've heard him say it seven thousand times. We remind ourselves of this timeless principle in all our communication, whether we're creating media pieces, writing an all-church letter, planning a song celebration, or writing connecting pieces for worship.

Great communication is always using words wisely and never overestimating the attention span of the listener. When I write, I put myself in the pew and think about what it would take to engage me, to give me enough information and inspiration to keep me connected, but not so much that I become bored. *Less is more.*

A COMMON LANGUAGE

Learning to craft worship segments to maximize connection is a process, but the key for me was learning to speak what I call Ginghamese. Every church needs a language that evolves out of its DNA. For instance, we don't have volunteers at Ginghamsburg; we have unpaid servants. We don't hold worship services; we prepare for worship celebrations. We try to use regular language and avoid "churchy" words. We use active, persuasive verbs. We keep it positive; we never resort to guilt-inducing verbal techniques. We say "us" and "we" instead of "me" and "you." We affirm. We try to draw attention to God and God's unpaid servants rather than the speakers on the stage. With words, we tell people that they are accepted; they are us. Words tell people that with God, there is no male or female, Jew or Greek, black or white, young or old—that we all have a place at the table of God.

I encourage you to reflect on your church's DNA and consider the language choices that might best support it. Language is important!

INTEGRATING THE PIECES

To ensure that multisensory worship connects with participants, we must take extra time to pull the pieces together. This is more artistically known as *integration*. Our team describes this connection in several ways: *terrific transitions, smooth segues, setting one another up, handing it off.*

Even though we might have exceptional individual pieces, if something is not in the right spot at the right time, if there is no context for why it is being presented, or if any segment is preceded or followed by a dead spot, its effectiveness can be lost. Multisensory worship is integrated worship; pieces overlap. Each piece builds on the last and prepares for the next.

Different teams will have different ways of engaging in the integration process. At Ginghamsburg, the team draws up the initial worship plans on the Plexiglas on Wednesday in the war room. It is essential, however, for someone to wrestle with those plans during the week; to try and imagine himself or herself in the room, thinking how it will look, feel, and connect. I like projecting out in this fashion, and a number of times I remember my husband saying to me, "How *was* worship this coming weekend?" He knew that in a sense I'd been there already! Team players must ask themselves questions during the course of the week, such as:

- How will that *feel*?
- How will it *feel* to have that rock song blast out of nowhere?
- How will it *feel* to bow in a prayer of confession when I don't yet realize I've done anything wrong?

- How effective will it *feel* to have an altar call for salvation when the message was about reaching out to serve others?

Part of designing worship to be multisensory means unlearning the way we've always done it. As we move toward integration, we've got to unlearn the way we've always considered various worship pieces as separate units. Separate pieces allow time for distraction. We want the pictures and stories to speak for themselves. If we lose our audience due to a distraction or a dead spot, it takes twenty minutes to get them back fully. We don't have twenty minutes to give away in any given worship celebration. Integrated, seamless worship eliminates distraction.

Maximizing each moment is essential. Here are some ways you can maximize the worship experience by integrating the pieces:

- Provide the host or worship leader with prepared lines that close one segment ("Amen. . . . It's good to worship together") and segue into the next ("Coming up, some Lenten opportunities you'll want to know about . . .").
- Choose the best times for the congregation to stand and sit. Avoid the "up and down" syndrome.
- Use lighting to enhance the most important worship element happening at any given time. (Be sure to transition smoothly between elements.)
- Advise stage participants about the best times to approach or leave the stage so they don't distract or create dead spots.
- Instead of saying, "We have a *video*," or "We have a *video* of that story," say, "Let's watch that story together," or "Check out what our mission group was able to do." No need to call attention to the fact that it's a video.
- Fade the audio out of the end of a movie clip, but leave the video on the screen as live music begins. (This is very effective!)
- Encourage the band to work through transitions ahead of time so that the musical flow is not interrupted.
- Tie the words spoken for the communion celebration into the overall theme of the worship celebration.
- Play a bit of appropriate music to set up and "bookend" a drama.
- Play soft music under prayers to help soften hearts.

Here's the deal—integration is *free*! It costs nothing in dollars and cents. You can begin integrating your pieces this week! Small churches and large churches have equal ability to integrate their worship, and it makes *all* the difference in the world.

PARTICIPATION OVERCOMING PERFORMANCE

As the Ginghamsburg congregation moved into the new millennium, we noticed that the ground was shifting beneath our worship paradigm. We realized our people had a greater need to *belong* than to be struck by our stage work. *All* people are on a search to be accepted, a quest to know that their thoughts, opinions, actions, service, experiences, and lives are important and useful. People need to know that we care before they will care what we know about rolling out great music, media, or even terrific messages.

As a result, we've made a 180-degree turn as we've worked to increase opportunities for overall participation in the worship celebrations. Here are some examples of what a pastor or worship host might say to make worship more participatory:

- "Turn to the person next to you and share an experience you've had with . . ."
- "Let's say this prayer out loud together as it comes up on the screen."
- "Let's stand to worship in song, and on your way up, greet someone and say how great it is to see him or her here today."
- "Stand up and say the name of the person who first introduced you to Jesus."
- "Speak out loud the first name of someone who needs our prayers today."

When time is limited, invitations like these provide an opportunity for everyone to participate simultaneously. When we have a little more time in the celebration, we invite people to pray or talk together in small groups. We never used to do this in the days of the megachurch movement, but now we're seeing that postmodern people want it, need it, and respond very well to it—even if at first it doesn't feel natural. It's like taking medicine. You hate it going down, but afterward you feel so much better! People may need a little help breaking out of their shells, but when they do, they feel so glad that they've connected. Although ours is a large church, we do our best to make sure that everyone is included during these discussion and prayer times.

Smaller churches have the edge on the participation piece. It's much easier to engage a smaller group of people in worship and community. Larger churches may be tempted to ride on performance, but a one-way conversation cannot engage people over the long haul. In any size church, we must make an intentional effort to reach out and make worship personal, to see the congregation not as one large mass of humanity but as unique individuals coming to find health and life in Jesus. The rewards are great when we allow participation to overcome performance.

CHAPTER 10

POWERFUL PRAYERS FOR EVERYDAY PEOPLE

*That's the kind of people the
Father is out looking for: those
who are simply and honestly
themselves before him in
their worship.*

—John 4:23, The Message

Prayer is two-way communication with God. Inside every celebration we are sure to hear a word *from* God. We traditionally call this the *message* or the *sermon*. In multisensory worship, we often enhance this word with a video story, a song (poetry of the culture), a well-planned live interview, or even some sort of drama. No matter how we've heard *from* God, however, we always create a time to talk *to* God. These prayers can take on myriad forms, as imaginative as our minds can allow.

As worship designers, we must place ourselves in the hearts and lives of the worshipers. With wisdom and compassion, we are called to give oral framing to what participants might desire to say to God in response to what they've experienced in worship. As we seek to guide the practice of prayer in worship, we must prepare well (perhaps by spending time in prayer ourselves), knowing that participants may need help articulating what is in their hearts and minds.

Prayer is simply talking to God, and prayer in worship is simply talking to God on behalf of the gathered faith community. On the following pages, you'll find examples of prayers we've used in our worship celebrations. Some were written for holidays or particular occasions. Others are simply everyday prayers, suitable for any worship gathering. While you may use these prayers in your worship, the most powerful prayers will be the ones you write—prayers created and spoken from the heart that God has given you for your people . . . amen.

Theme: Pursuing the Dream

Occasion: Dr. Martin Luther King Jr. Weekend

Desired outcome: Participants will become part of the authentic community that will relentlessly pursue the dream of a multicultural kingdom.

Background: At the close of the message, three worship participants (a diverse trio) led the following prayer together

Leaders: "We know God has called us to demonstrate the multicultural kingdom . . . and we know we're not there yet. God is calling us to pursue the dream harder than ever, whatever the cost. Let's stand together to say this prayer of intention as it appears on the screen."

Prayer:
We have a dream . . .
To be a faith community that fully demonstrates the call of Jesus
Where people of all ages, genders, cultures,
All backgrounds, and economic statuses are welcomed.
Where God's love breaks down the wall of racial barriers,
Personal preferences, and preconceived notions about others.
Where we lay down our pride and prejudice,
Our fear of difference, and our burden of sin.
And where we fully demonstrate the
Unnatural, unconditional, and undeniable love of God.
Together we say, "Thy kingdom come,
Thy will be done on earth as it is in heaven."
This is our dream. Amen.

Theme: One Heart & Soul

Occasion: Any

Desired outcome: Participants will realize the presence and blessing of God that come only in community.

Background: As preparation before a message in a series about authentic community, we led this time of participation and prayer.

one heart and soul: authentic community

Host: "We all face the same challenge . . . to find a community of people we truly like, who feel safe and inviting, who will draw us closer to God. We all have fears, anxieties about meeting people and connecting to community. I know I do! But ultimately, most of us wouldn't be here today if we didn't want the full presence of God in our lives.

"What brought you to this place of community, and what keeps you here? Love? Jesus? Spirit? Music? Truth?" (Ask for out-loud, one-word responses from the congregation—it helps to make them comfortable responding.)

"Thanks for your response. Psalm 133 says, 'How good and pleasant it is when brothers and sisters dwell together in unity . . . for there the Lord shares his blessing, even life forevermore.' Let's pray this prayer together as it appears on the screen."

Prayer:
Lord, we've come for a variety of reasons:
To find hope and healing,
To give our kids hope and direction,
To discover a place of love and acceptance,
And to live out your call in our lives.
Today we ask for courage and strength
To reach out beyond ourselves
In order to truly become part of the kingdom of God,
The Authentic Community.
Most of all, today we want
To give you honor and glory
By giving you all of who we are.
We give you our hearts and our souls.
Have your way in our lives, Jesus. Amen.

Theme: Resurrection—Alive Again!

Occasion: Easter

Desired outcome: Participants will stand up and (figuratively) move forward in the power of the resurrection.

Background: Easter brings a lot of guests to worship celebrations. We try to design a celebration of hope, careful to include some pieces that might feel familiar to the guests. For our prayer aloud together, we said the Lord's Prayer, since many who grew up in church are familiar with it. People seem to truly appreciate and feel more at home when they can genuinely participate.

Later, following the resurrection story of Mike Martindale, we asked Mike to come up to the stage. (Mike suffered a stroke and survived a three-month coma after an accident on a three-wheeler. His story is included on the Redesigning Worship Companion DVD, available through the Ginghamsburg Web store.) The congregation gave him a standing ovation. I then told Mike how much he and his story meant to us, and I asked him to pray. It was such a powerful moment, and something that Mike could do for us and with us. Here is the prayer we wrote for Mike to speak.

Prayer:

Lord . . . thank you for new life.
Thank you for each day we share.
Thank you for your amazing love
That is shown through all creation
And through the people you've put in our lives.
This day belongs to you,
And we give you all the honor and glory. Amen.

Theme: The Best Godly Man Show, Period.

Occasion: Father's Day weekend

Desired outcome: Male participants will actively take their places as men of God. Female participants will support them as they take this step of faith.

Background: We did this entire celebration in the style of the popular

sports show on cable television. Leather couches, coffee cups, and men sitting on the couches discussing the challenges of being Christlike men, husbands, and dads. Our pastor led the discussion and then, at the close of this creative celebration, asked all the men in the room to stand and say this prayer of promise out loud together as it appeared on the screen.

Prayer:
Father God, we stand before you today,
Challenged to take our place as men of God,
Passionate in our pursuit of you.
We confess to allowing ourselves to be tamed,
Forgetting the mission that you have called us
To take on as your disciples.
Hear our prayer as we seek the strength
To flee distraction, to pursue integrity,
To fight the good fight, to take hold of your call on our lives
And the lives of those we love.
This we ask because of you,
Our mighty God, our passionate Father.
In Jesus' name, amen.

Theme: Dad Almighty

Occasion: Father's Day or any other occasion

Desired outcome: Participants will embrace and enjoy the love of their heavenly Father.

Background: We often use video clips from movies to introduce an entire worship celebration or to make a point within the message. We found a video clip from the movie *Smoke Signals*, but it didn't seem to fit in either of those places. When I saw it, I realized it would set up the prayer in a powerful way. The clip is video footage of a huge river flowing vigorously between rock and mountain formations. The voiceover is a man, reflecting on his own father experience. "Shall we forgive our fathers?" he starts out, then continues with a monologue that would catch the heart of any adult.

Coming out of that clip (with soft, live piano music in the background), I spoke these words to our people.

Leader: "Shall we forgive our fathers? How shall we understand a heavenly Father who seeks to love, discipline, care for, and give generously to each of his children every day? Is our understanding of Dad Almighty totally dependent on our experience of Dad-so-earthly—our human fathers?

"The truth today for all of us is that, yes, we must forgive. For if we never understand and receive the love and amazing grace of this heavenly Father, we can never be truly transformed in Christ. We will at best be lost children, gazing longingly through the glass at others who have learned the love and acceptance of Dad Almighty, yet settling for never knowing it ourselves. We go about our lives pretending to be loved, but not truly knowing and feeling it on the inside. Will you bow your heads and pray with me now?"

Prayer (*host prays*): "Forgive us, Father, for we've tried to live our lives by numbly assenting to faith, rather than courageously renewing our minds with the acceptance and assurance of the powerful love you have for each one of us. 'How great is the love the Father has lavished on us, that we should be called the children of God,' your children. May our time with you today change our hearts and minds toward renewal and health. Amen."

Theme: Spirit of Faith

Occasion: Blessing of the Bikes event

Desired outcome: Participants will move out of their zones of comfort, to live with a pioneering, risk-taking spirit.

Background: We have a Broken Chains motorcycle ministry at Ginghamsburg that annually hosts a motorcycle outreach event. Bikers from all over are invited to come for an outdoor tent event including a local ride, a "splash" water blessing for each bike, and a special worship celebration. We discovered that bikers are passionate about their lifestyle and hobby, and there is a definite spiritual connection that can be captured through such an event. Here is the blessing we spoke over each bike as it was blessed:

Blessing of the Bikes:

May the road ahead be safe.

May all your turns be smooth.

May your feet always find solid ground,

And may the Spirit of Faith always ride with you.

Go with God's wind. Amen.

PART IV: MULTIPLYING MULTISENSORY WORSHIP

A s a missional church, Ginghamsburg has identified a core business of transformational discipleship: making disciples, spreading the word, and serving others. If there were three Rs to describe this call as it pertains to worship, they would be *relevance*, *relationships*, and *rigorous mission*. Healthy organisms grow, and healthy churches will be fertile soil for new gardens of fruitful growth.

In Mark 2 we read the story of a man who wasn't physically able to get himself into the home where Jesus was teaching. His friends put together a plan to lower him through the roof because the home was so crowded they couldn't get in the door. It's the same sort of "crowd chaos" that presents a barrier for our churches today. How can we keep welcoming new people into our churches when the crowd is so intimidating? And how can we create welcoming spaces for seekers who have been turned off or turned out by traditional Christianity?

This was to be Ginghamsburg's great commission, our next call from God—creating new worship communities and providing more places than ever for servants to serve!

CHAPTER 11

ALTERNATIVE WORSHIP COMMUNITIES

Everyone I meet—it matters little whether they're mannered or rude, smart or simple—deepens my sense of interdependence and obligation . . . [proclaiming] God's powerful plan to rescue everyone who trusts him, starting with Jews and then right on to everyone else!

—Paul, Romans 1:14-16, The Message

Have you ever had a lightbulb moment? An awareness of truth that turned everything in your comfortable little world upside down? One of my most profound lightbulb moments came as a result of several transitions within the Ginghamsburg community several years ago. During that season, I discovered that change can be channeled as positive momentum. Healthy organisms embrace change—even if something is not yet broken. And while "big worship" or conventional worship as we know it was not yet broken, we found ourselves needing to explore alternative forms of weekly worship. What kind of gathering might the body of Christ be moving toward? How might we best facilitate growth and dynamic life for followers of Jesus now while effectively preparing ourselves for the days to come?

In the early 2000s our pastor, Mike Slaughter, felt strongly that in light of our call to serve and pour out our resources on behalf of others in the world, we could not justify the expense of building new worship facilities. In fact, Mike determined that for as long as possible we would focus our ministry efforts on discipleship and social action rather than spend our resources on buildings that decay. This concept became known and repeated among the Ginghamsburg church family as . . .

"MINIMIZE BRICK, MAXIMIZE MISSION"

"Minimize brick" meant that whatever problems arose, we were not going to solve them by building more space. This meant that the "kids" would have to share the toys and the rooms and get along. This meant that ministries could no longer claim sole ownership of campus classrooms. This meant that every inch of space would need to be utilized to the fullest degree, requiring constant rearrangement. "Maximize mission" meant that the mission would come first, and thus all of us would need to know and understand the mission very well in order to fulfill it. This meant that to multiply our worship numbers (healthy organisms grow), we would need to think about multiplying venues, not seats in an auditorium.

During that time, we stumbled onto startling statistics claiming that megachurches as we knew them would be obsolete in ten years and that we must be prepared to convert our thinking . . .

Beyond Bigger Crowds to Better Connection

I've heard it said that for the most part, it's leaders who like crowds, not the people in those crowds. Most people prefer to be treated as individuals and given a customized experience, not herded like cows and spoken to as invisible entities. Connection lines tend to be stronger when there are fewer people in the room and when those people have names and faces and personalities. This would help pave the way to greater intimacy in worship.

Beyond Performance to Participation

We are becoming a much more interactive culture. People like to participate by doing more than singing a few songs. The people in our communities have stories to share, responses to give, and issues to face. What could happen if we began our collective discussions during our worship experience? What if we allowed time to talk out loud and truly get to know the people around us? But who will be the ones to start and lead these congregational conversations? We currently have only three paid clergy at Ginghamsburg, for a church of more than four thousand. Clearly, the time has come to go . . .

Beyond Paid Staff to the Priesthood of All Believers

Jesus-followers naturally want to serve in meaningful ways. The volunteers of today are sophisticated and time starved. When people carve out time to serve, we want to them to be able to do something life changing and significant. We all know people in our churches who, while they may not be skilled to speak to a crowd of one thousand, can certainly be engaging hosts or greeters in a smaller venue. When we divide ourselves into smaller worshiping communities, we open up a whole new set of significant servant roles to be carried out week after week after week. In this smaller worship environment, the community feeling overtakes any tendency to focus on performance. It's a call to go . . .

Beyond Excellence to Experience

In the 1990s we heard a lot of talk about excellence in worship. It seemed necessary at the time to jump-start us to much better and more effective means of sharing the gospel with a lost world. But there is something people crave more than excellence, and that is experience. People want to come to church and *experience* God in some way. Perhaps through a song or a message or a prayer or a welcoming face, but people want and need a memorable experience, not "I came, I worshiped, I left—unchanged."

And so our lightbulb moment became a collective realization that, rather than financially strap the next generation with a huge building and subsequent mortgage, we would max out the use of our current facilities. This led to our consideration of what some are calling the multi-site movement, the innovation of what we now call alternative worship communities.

We were hesitant at first—literally starting in the dark (as is our norm), stepping out to use only who and what we had. We began to dream and project what an alternative worship venue could look like at Ginghamsburg where we had one style of worship that was eclectic and inclusive and everyone seemed to enjoy. We asked, "What would it take to entice people out of *big* worship into a celebration where they would potentially watch the weekend message on video? What could we do in this worship gathering that we couldn't logistically do in the bigger, conventional worship setting? And how might we reach out into another segment of the culture in a unique and tangible way?" Several years and significant hindsight later, we have launched and are hosting a variety of alternative worship communities each week. Here is a brief description of each one:

NEXT STEP: A WORSHIP CELEBRATION FOR PEOPLE ON THE ROAD TO RECOVERY

Ginghamsburg already had a counseling program and a growing recovery community in place. We had support groups for various addictions and life situations. What we didn't have was a customized worship experience designed just for the people in these programs. Since part of our DNA is to "grow hope one life at a time"—and most of our weekend messages carry a great word of hope—it seemed right to  inject this piece of our DNA into the recovery community. Checking our weekend calendar, we identified that a Saturday evening time could be open and would work well for those in need of sobriety. We discussed how we might open space in the main worship area by removing chairs from the back—providing safe space for community conversations before and after the worship time, eliminating any need to be wandering the halls. We acknowledged that Jesus charged us with searching the highways and byways and admonished his disciples that it was sick persons who needed a doctor, so we stepped out in faith to see what God might do. I put together a focus team at the onset—several recoverees with leadership gifts—and we met weekly for a month to plan the content, style of music, and community support for this celebration, the most unique additional factor being a weekly story of recovery written and shared by a different person each week.

Easter weekend of 2005 we rolled out plans for our very first Next Step worship celebration, to be officially launched the following weekend. View one person's story of recovery, shown to our Ginghamsburg community as we lifted up the vision for that celebration to our church family. (See Redesigning Worship Companion DVD.)

NEXT STEP @ NOON

Once we'd launched the Next Step celebration, the movement became contagious. Nearly three hundred people now gather each  Saturday night at seven o'clock for this whoopin' and hollerin' time of celebration. These people realize they are broken, rest in their Redeemer, and cheer on one another toward the high call of Christ Jesus! Jay Meyer (whose recovery story is featured on the Redesigning Worship Companion DVD) is one of the lead lay pastors of this community, and after seeing this groundswell of response, he seized the idea of a lunchtime recovery venue. If the message was already on DVD, why couldn't we hold a "brown bag" worship where folks could stop in during their workday, view a portion of the weekend message, and talk together about their current journey of faith? Next Step @ Noon was launched, and it has become a weekly watering hole for thirsty recoverees. Inside the safe space of our ARK gathering room (our classy but comfortable original country church building that is now remodeled and media friendly) they sit on couches or at café tables, eat lunch, and listen or talk together. Once the message and dialogue are over, communion is served. In a final moment of gratitude, these worshipers join hands in a circle and say the Lord's Prayer together. Next Step @ Noon is a powerful experience, which is open to anyone needing workday refreshment.

MONDAY NIGHT WORSHIP @ THE ARK

This next alternative worship venue was invented as we wondered if some of our longtime attendees might be looking for a

smaller, more intimate church feeling, simpler acoustic worship music, and hymns.
We pictured a setting where young parents
would feel welcome to bring their children
into the worship and weekend travelers
could return home and get their
Ginghamsburg worship "fix" on any given
week. Overall, this venue could appeal to

folks who felt attached to the smaller, more traditional church atmosphere but who embraced Ginghamsburg's message and mission.

Thus was born Monday Night Worship @ the ARK. At 6:30 on
any Monday evening you will find these worshipers helping themselves to fresh, hot coffee-shop offerings in the back of the room, after
which they are welcomed by an unpaid host pastor. The host and worship leader who lead this venue are live, but the previous weekend's
message is offered via DVD. It is definitely a smaller church feel, culminating in communion every week at the close of the message. This
gathering has been significant in creating new connections of life
transformation!

SUNDAY CAFÉ

With the Monday Night
Worship tucked under our belts we
felt ready to start a similar experience on Sunday mornings during
the most popular worship time on
our main campus, 10:15. A third
worship area was available, the

large gathering room in our south campus discipleship center (also
housing our New Path Ministries, food pantry, and counseling center),
and we were anxious to create a more cafélike environment in
that setting.

We briefly advertised this alternative worship option among our
church family, stating that we were seeking mission-driven
Ginghamsburg attendees who for any number of reasons desired a
smaller, more relational worship community. A coffee bar laden with
fresh hot coffee, tea, and breakfast rolls greets these guests, and great

conversation is the goal for this venue from start to finish. Two host pastor couples take turns leading the top of the worship celebration along with a small band playing slightly more upbeat worship songs than the acoustic offering of Monday nights. The exact same weekend message is viewed via DVD (edited Saturday night), and all the week-end updates are shared often via prepared video.

GATEWAY CAFÉ

New Path, Inc., is the outreach arm of Ginghamsburg Church. New Path servants are a force to be reckoned with. They *love* lifting up

the least of these, whether by restor-ing and delivering furniture, repair-ing vehicles to give away, collecting and sorting food for hungry people, or locating housing for those who have no place to call home. New Path servants have always found a way to make it happen and fulfill the need, whatever the case may be.

The time came, however, when the New Path servants felt it no longer seemed enough to simply hand out groceries to the Monday night families. Their collective vision grew, and they came up with the idea of serving up a restaurant-style dinner and a message along with the bags of groceries. Many prayers and planning sessions later, Gateway Café became a reality. It's Gateway because this weekly Monday night gathering truly serves as a gateway to hope, a pathway into the larger arms of the Ginghamsburg community.

The evening flows something like this: between 4:30 and 5:00, families begin streaming into our Main Campus lobby (Gateway quickly outgrew it's original, smaller Discipleship Center location) and find their way to servants stationed and prepared to sign them up for various physical needs, such as groceries, furniture, household goods, Christmas gifts, and so on. From the lobby these folks are wel-comed into the food service lines where Ginghamsburg cell groups dish up delicious, hot, home-cooked meals and words of welcome. Moms, dads, children, and grandparents are then seated family style at large round tables set up in the main worship area. Music is playing and the stage is set beautifully, just as for weekend worship. Delighted chatter floats through the air until a worship leader sings a song that leads into a brief, live version of the weekend message. A teary-eyed communion exchange culminates this time of worship, and it's apparent that servants and guests alike are blessed. Gateway Café is growing hope and health, one life at a time. (View the story of Gateway Café's inception on the Redesigning Worship Companion DVD.)

WHERE DO WE GO FROM HERE?

Alternative worship communities by no means negate the need to create powerful God experiences in the larger setting. We use those carefully crafted pieces from the conventional worship program and translate them into customized versions for each of these venues. The result is a signature Ginghamsburg worship celebration in a variety of styles, meeting a wide array of physical, spiritual, and emotional needs. Through the power of replicated media and multiple servant teams, we are able to extend our reach farther than we ever dreamed possible. Consider this list for starting your own alternative worship community:

First Steps: Strategic Ownership and Leadership

Who are the people you are targeting for this worship celebration? The best leaders are those who, out of their personal experience, are now passionate about reaching this community. Jay Meyer is a recovering drug and alcohol addict. Sherry Canfarelli, who helps lead the Gateway community, was a single mom greatly in need of physical and emotional support. These are the kinds of leaders who will hang in there and make it happen. Start by identifying a focus group of these folks who will become the team that deploys the venue. Once this focus group begins to meet, identify the various leaders and address these additional important issues:

Pastor-Host (we call this person *the face with the place*)

This must be a contagious person (or persons) who can take direction and coaching but who ultimately has the gift of leadership and "follow-ability"; a spiritually mature person with a heart for ministry.

Music

The music must fit the style of the community. Talk through what this would ideally look and sound like, then seek out a music leader who can execute this customized style of music.

Greeters and Facilitators

All kinds of friendly people can join in and welcome guests. Be sure to have an experienced person train this team to help them offer amazing grace and huge "hellos"!

Food-Hospitality Team

Most alternative venues have a refreshment component (remember, there was usually food wherever Jesus hung out). Initially discuss all the hopes and dreams for radical hospitality and decide who will be responsible for what. Be sure to have enough people on this team so that no one person gets burned out trying to take care of the weekly tasks involved.

Children's Activities

We like to offer meaningful, age-appropriate children's activities at every worship time. The children grow in faith, and in turn, their parents are well served and able to fully experience their own moments with God. Partner with your children's ministry by casting the vision and working together to assure this important aspect of your community.

Support Systems (location, setup, tear-down, etc.)

Never overlook the logistics involved with each individual worship gathering or assume that everyone understands the work involved. Map it out, recruit a team, and enjoy the execution. Yes, there are some people whom God has wired to thrive while carrying out these physical acts of service!

Test Pilot

Whenever a new, weekly worship celebration is developed, it is a good idea to hold at least one test pilot experience. Invite close friends or family to sit in as an audience, and ask for feedback when it's over. In a very real way, worship is one of those events in which you might not get a second chance to make a good first impression. First-time guests will have an expectation that what they see and experience on any given week is what they can expect every week. This is not a good time to wing it; rather, make sure you and your team give it your absolute best shot.

Whenever I speak and share about alternative worship communities, I like to close by asking this interactive invention question: Pretend Jesus walked up to you today and said you have a short time to live. Before you make that final trip heavenward, you are charged with creating a worship venue that doesn't already exist for people who aren't being reached in your community. What would it look like? Where would be the best location? What style of music would you go for? What additional components might you add to this worship gathering? Who might lead this alternative worship experience?

Challenge yourself to think outside the box, and consider Jesus' call to the missionary in all of us. The blessings will outweigh the work, and you will know the thrill of God's using your life for kingdom advancement.

CHAPTER 12

THE TEAMS SURROUNDING THE TEAM: SERVING IN COMMUNITY

Now the body is not made up of one part but of many.
                              —Paul, 1 Corinthians 12:14

Part of Ginghamsburg's core DNA is the belief that each person in the church is called to service. For some of us, that service is also our vocation, our paid employment. Others serve faithfully without pay, but with equal effectiveness. To recognize the importance of this service, we refer to these workers as unpaid servants. We're a large church, so we have many hundreds of unpaid servants in every area of ministry who have signed on to be a part of the music, media, or worship enhancement teams. Without them, we couldn't do worship the way we do it.

So far we've explored the job descriptions of the core worship design team players and discussed the ways each one contributes to the dreaming and development stages of worship design. But remember, great teams don't just dream and develop together. They also deploy, and deployment requires a larger team. At Ginghamsburg the larger team is filled out with unpaid servants. Each week, some of the development and nearly *all* of the deployment are carried out by unpaid servants who've been engaged in this mission. Here's a little bit about who they are and how they serve.

UNPAID SERVANTS IN MEDIA MINISTRY

Integral to the weekend worship's media ministry are these technical, unpaid team players:

Floor Director

This person is the eyes of the worship area and gives the weekend director that particular perspective. The floor director also helps the team to anticipate changes in the worship order, content, or plans. He or she assures the timeliness of the various huddles and tech meetings that take place, keeping everyone on schedule throughout the weekend.

Weekend Director

This person is the captain of the live screen. From the vantage point of the media loft, this person is in charge of directing what goes on the screen and when.

Technical Director

This person executes the weekend director's commands via the video mixer.

Camera Operators

These four people run the live cameras for image magnification and additional visual communication.

Audio Technicians

These persons are trained to assist in all worship venues and events, setting up and running sound, media, or technical equipment.

All media team members maintain continuous communication and are connected through the headset miking system.

Servant teams for worship ministry are large and diverse. To offer a closer look inside the various servant roles, we asked a few Ginghamsburg servants to share what this opportunity has meant in their lives.

SERVANT SNAPSHOT: LUCAS HALL

How I serve: As a part of the Ginghamsburg Media Ministry I run floor camera for at least one weekend of worship celebrations a month.

How I got here: I'm a senior in high school now, but five years ago I approached Todd Carter [Ginghamsburg's chief media producer at the time] about serving. Todd was a role model for me in the media sense, and even though I wasn't quite old enough, he let me start—and I have been running camera ever since. Since then I've become more involved and learned to serve in other media positions as well.

What I love most: I love being involved. I love being able to do God's work—invisibly. Everyone can see your camera shot or the video playing on the screen, but to the congregation, it just appears. I like that I helped put it there but that no one saw me do it, or even has to think twice about how the media got onto the screen.

What's happened to me: Serving in media has ultimately shaped what I want to do with my life, and I am now pursuing a future in media design. I started a film club at my high school to help other kids get involved—they don't just learn how to run a camera or make a video but gain some background knowledge using some basic production rules. When Todd let me in as an underage kid, he couldn't have known how he would shape my life. Media has allowed me to effectively serve in a way that others benefit— in a behind-the-scenes kind of way.

SERVANT SNAPSHOT: STEVE WRIGHT

How I serve: I am part of the Ginghamsburg Technical Team, primarily serving as a remote setup specialist. I help wherever and whenever I'm asked—for adult events and sometimes student/children's events as well.

How I got here: We learned about Ginghamsburg from people in our small town—adults and students—talking about this "big church." We felt welcomed right from the start, and the first couple of messages really hit home for us. We'd been attending Ginghamsburg for about six months, and I was looking for a place to get involved and serve. I decided to stop in and offer my service to the director of music and media, Paul Jones. Not long after that, Kim invited me to serve as the weekly remote specialist for the Sunday Café worship venue at our south campus.

What I love most: I have learned to know a lot of people—and that would not have happened if I'd never offered to serve. Serving has connected my wife and me to this church. You just need to start somewhere and get involved.

What's happened to me: I enjoy this church a lot, but if it weren't for my servant role, I just wouldn't feel connected. A recent mission trip to New Orleans was another great experience for us, and we are still getting together with friends we made on that trip. We also have a cell group that meets in our home. Something would definitely be missing from my life if I weren't serving!

SERVANT SNAPSHOT: SIDNEY TRAYNHAM

How I serve: During my time at Ginghamsburg I wore quite a few hats—everything from coordinating worship for our recovery community to traveling as a videographer into Darfur, Sudan. Somewhere in between I did a whole lot of media production, worship planning, and graphic design.

How I got here: I was the ultimate Ginghamsburg groupie. I first went to a Ginghamsburg conference during my college years not knowing what to expect, and I walked away totally astounded at the passion, creativity, and vision found at a church within my own United Methodist denomination. So, I kept coming back to conference after conference until I was invited to be an unpaid summer intern—which, little did I realize, was just the beginning.

What I love most: It feels selfish to say I loved the euphoria and high that come from witnessing thousands of people laughing, crying, and growing because of our work designing worship. I am not sure there are many other jobs where you get to see that kind of massive affirmation and feedback on a weekly basis. But even more, I loved witnessing an entire church so passionately unifying around a single mission—hunger relief in Darfur, for example—and to observe how this mission became the single, greatest thing happening in the lives of thousands of Ginghamsburg servants and beyond.

What's happened to me: As much as I absolutely love creative arts and the rhythm of weekly worship, I ultimately was called to leave that world. Because of my encounters with issues of justice, poverty, and sacrificial mission during my time at Ginghamsburg, I took a position in a church-based humanitarian relief and development organization. Still, one of the most important values I learned and practiced at Ginghamsburg was the power of human stories—which is absolutely critical to the work that we now do overseas.

UNPAID SERVANTS IN MUSIC MINISTRY

Music ministry is crucial to any church movement, and the faithful, devoted ministry servant teams are absolutely essential. Thankfully, this ministry area is a great magnet for unpaid servants who have amazing and anointed musical gifts to share. Periodically, we advertise or announce that we are auditioning vocalists and instrumentalists for our music ministry. It is up to the servant to decide how often he or she wants to be scheduled, as each weekend is a large time commitment. Most serve one or two weekends each month, and in serving they find that the music ministry often becomes their place of relational community.

The key players we regularly schedule are keyboards, drums, bass, electric and acoustic guitar, and of course, vocalists. But I don't know of any instrument that we'd refuse to use. On various occasions we've included violin, saxophone, double bass, hand percussion, and even a rain stick. Change-ups are good!

SERVANT SNAPSHOT: JOHN WAGNER

How I serve: Lead vocalist in the Ginghamsburg Music Ministry.

How I got here: A Ginghamsburg couple invited me to come to church with them. They thought I might fit well into the music ministry—and they were right!

What I love most: I love our slightly unorthodox pastor, our style of worship, and the teaching and preaching of Ginghamsburg Church. I love knowing that I am a part of a global community that's making a positive difference in a world torn apart. I also love being a part of a church family that prays and is quick to respond to the needs of others.

What's happened to me: I'm learning more, loving more, following better, and waiting when necessary. Using my gifts has helped me to work out my salvation.

SERVANT SNAPSHOT: ANGIE CHRONISTER

How I serve: Lead vocalist in the Ginghamsburg Music Ministry.

How I got here: After attending Ginghamsburg for a while I spotted an ad in the bulletin to come and sing in the choir. I have always had a passion for singing and realized this could be a fun way to join in.

What I love most: At first I thought singing on the large stage might come across as superficial, but once I became part of this ministry it felt like a true community where everyone cared for one another. I always liked helping others, and this ministry feels very missional to me. We touch others in a tangible way through worship. The actual singing is really a small part of a larger connection, a community where everyone cares for one another.

What's happened to me: Some people have a hard time understanding how we can put in such long weekend hours (eleven total weekend hours once a month), but for me this is about the mission of Jesus and helping other people in their journey as well. I've experienced true worship at a different level than ever before.

SERVANT SNAPSHOT: SHAWN ALLEN

How I serve: Lead electric guitarist in the Ginghamsburg Band.

How I got here: I wasn't part of Ginghamsburg Church at all when one day a musician friend called and invited me to audition for the band at Ginghamsburg. I then became an occasional player and now serve and attend more on a regular basis.

What I love most: I really like the high level of commitment that's expected here at Ginghamsburg, and also the high bar for musical quality. I appreciate that we aren't called to just show up, but rather we push each other to the next level musically and it brings out the best in all of us.

What's happened to me: Since being part of this ministry, I've connected with people and developed many friendships. I've been enlightened to see how many ways people can serve at this church—everything from stage assistants to kitchen cooks to custodians. It's amazing.

SERVANT SNAPSHOT: MARCIA TERRELL-SPARKS

How I serve: Vocalist with the Ginghamsburg Music Ministry.

How I got here: I have always had a passion for singing. After a friend invited my husband and me to Ginghamsburg, we always made our way to the balcony where we could get a bird's-eye view of everything going on in the worship celebrations. A young woman who sat near us encouraged me to come and sing in the choir. A year later, when I finally walked into a choir rehearsal, that same young woman lit up and told me I'd really enjoy it . . . and I do!

What I love most: I love everything about the worship experience: the heartfelt songs, the visual themes with backdrops, props, artwork, and colors. Most of all I love that the word of God speaks to my heart each week.

What's happened to me: I need to feel connected to others and to interact with the people of God. Serving in the music ministry helps me to grow and be spiritually involved as well as to open myself to pray for others. I enjoy watching how God shines through each of us as we deliver the songs of praise in each worship celebration.

UNPAID SERVANTS IN OTHER WORSHIP AREAS

Remember, part of Ginghamsburg's mission statement is "to serve out of our Call and giftedness." Our church leadership truly affirms serving and giving as genuine acts of worship. In support of this affirmation, each year we update our Servant Role Catalog that describes hundreds of unpaid servant positions, much like a user-friendly classified employment section. (See www.ginghamsburg.org/serveothers/.) Each attendee is challenged to fill out a servant form through an annual late-summer "Servant Series" of messages. Team leaders follow up with respondents quickly and train them well with evening or Saturday training sessions. These are hands-on opportunities to learn the jobs. Each servant starts out with a limited amount of responsibility. As he or she demonstrates competence, we increase the responsibility so that each one can be deployed effectively on mission.

While the music and media teams are large and extremely important to each week's celebrations, various other artists and collaborators also participate as servants in the weekly worship experience. When you count them up, it's a lot of people to keep connected! We knew that some of these additional worship contributors didn't necessarily need to meet on a weekly basis, but we wanted to stay in touch with them. So I began to pull together lists of people who had responded to an ad in the bulletin or our Servant Role Catalog, people wanting to serve out of their call and giftedness. We now usually communicate with these people online, with contact lists organized according to gifts and areas of desired service. Here are some examples:

- Actors on Call—experienced dramatic players of all ages who are willing to work within the challenges of our quick turn-around times.
- Artists Anonymous—artistic talents in all mediums: chalk, watercolor, interior design, ceramics, graphic design, and others.
- Photographers—experienced photographers who are willing to use their time and equipment to capture images for screen graphics or building décor.

- Researchers—information junkies who, when given the weekend theme, will send back great quotes and factoids that are then forwarded to the weekend speaker.

Besides enriching the worship experience, the additional media elements we incorporate into our worship celebrations create more opportunities to serve. Many people want to contribute, and now we have meaningful tasks to offer them. There's so much to do! One key role has been filled beautifully by a servant we've come to know as "Resurrection Mike."

Mike Martindale, whom I mentioned in chapter 10, had a miraculous recovery from a tragic accident at age sixteen (twenty years ago). Most weekends Mike makes himself available as an assistant to the entire worship team. There are always candles to be lit, water bottles to be fetched, cameras to be white-balanced, coffee to be secured. Mike stands by, ready to complete these tasks and myriad others. Truth be told, we couldn't do worship without Mike. Even if we could, we wouldn't want to. He's the worship cheerleader who passionately encourages us with his words and energy. Every church needs at least one Mike. His pay is the relationships we share and the meaning his servant role gives him.

I could tell story after story. There are so many ways to serve in a worship celebration that is multisensory, multimedia, and multicultural. And worship celebration is only the beginning—one way for servants to pursue their callings. At Ginghamsburg (and I'm sure in your church too) other ministry areas offer incredible opportunities for service. People can serve as members of the medic team, teen mentors in the dance club, coffee shop servers, or prayer counselors. Check out the possibilities at Ginghamsburg's website and then begin dreaming about your own. Worship team leaders have a unique and important role in guiding the church's worship, but the authentic community, in the end, creates powerful God experiences. It's incredible what God can do through passionate people!

PART V:
NOBODY TOLD ME THE
ROAD WOULD BE EASY

The road to creating powerful God experiences is seldom smooth. Like any project worth doing, worship design will always present its share of challenges, obstacles that try to keep us from seeing the promise ahead. At times we may feel like giving up. We may run out of money; we may not have enough help. We may get to a point that we simply feel too tired to continue. But if we keep our eyes fixed on our goal, if we remember that our results will have eternal consequences, if we trust our trials to God in prayer, we will eventually overcome. We have God's word on that.

Ten-plus years of serving in the same ministry area in the same church taught me a lot about perseverance. I've experienced failure and hardship. I've seen servants come and go. But God keeps working. Sometimes the best servant is the one who's just too dumb or too stubborn to let the obstacles stand in the way. Somewhere in my heart of hearts, I firmly believe that for every problem, God has a solution—and I'm just crazy enough to stick around to find out what it is!

In these final two chapters, I'd like to share some principles for overcoming obstacles you may encounter as a team and as a church movement, in the hope that you will learn to persevere through the hard times in order to design extraordinary God experiences.

CHAPTER 13
OVERCOMING OBSTACLES IN WORSHIP DESIGN

You must do the thing you think you cannot do.

—Eleanor Roosevelt

When church leaders attend our conferences, they inevitably want to know "the dirt" about our worship ministry—our greatest challenges, our worst mistakes, where we went wrong and how we corrected ourselves. Perhaps we all just need permission to fall down and scrape our knees, blow off the boo-boos, and get up and try again. Every worship planner needs to know that he or she is not alone. Yes, we all make mistakes, and Ginghamsburg team members are no exception.

No test or temptation that comes your way is beyond the course of what others have had to face. All you need to remember is that God will never let you down; he'll never let you be pushed past your limit; he'll always be there to help you come through it.

—1 Corinthians 10:13, The Message

CONFLICTS AS A CREATIVE FORCE

Conflict is a part of human life. As individuals, we have conflicting feelings inside ourselves. As groups, we experience conflict between people. All families experience interpersonal conflict from time to time, and creative teams should not be surprised when conflict arises. Verbal conflict can actually be a healthy sign that team members feel free to express what's going on inside them.

Assuming that team players embrace a shared set of values (a team or larger church mission statement, for example), they can remind one another of who they are and *whose* they are when conflict arises. We don't have to continually reinvent the wheel when we know who we are and what we're about. New ideas and creative suggestions can be examined through the lens of "Is this really *us*? Will this communicate effectively to *our* people?" As teams grow into and through this kind of process, the potential tension over *my* ideas versus *your* ideas can be greatly reduced. Instead, we all work together to seek out the *best* ideas based on the unique scenario of any given week.

Negative attitudes can persist, however. As a team, we strive to name any elephant (challenge or issue) that may be in the room as we meet. It's best to invite the affected team player to talk through what he or she might be thinking or feeling about the issue. Next, the entire team can join in to listen, care, reflect, and speak words of correction, hope, and healing. Occasionally, the team leader may need to speak with a team member privately about an obvious source of angst. A huge emotional release can occur as a result of simply talking things out. Best of all, this healthy team approach allows God to be bigger as the team grows in honesty and trust. Don't be afraid of team conflict. It can be a creative force that propels the team toward a new and deepened relationship.

DRY SPELLS IN WORSHIP DESIGN

No matter what ministry we're involved in, no matter what our day jobs might be, we all go through dry spells. Designing powerful God experiences week in and week out, fifty-two times a year, can be creatively exhausting. It's important to realize that we are human vessels housing a supernatural force, and that as human vessels, we must take the necessary steps to avoid burnout.

Dry spells in the team setting usually signal dry spells in the individual players' lives. When we allow ourselves to forgo daily personal time with God, a weekly day for re-creation, or a seasonal sabbath (vacation time), we put ourselves in a vulnerable position, susceptible to temptation, negative attitudes, burnout, and dry spells. But if we tend carefully to our life of faith, it's the Holy Spirit's responsibility to come through with the creative flow, and I've never known God to let us down.

Here are some ideas for re-creating yourself:

- Pick up a book with a creative or inspiring theme, and get *lost* in it.
- Visit an art gallery.
- Attend a conference that will stretch your ministry paradigm.
- Take a walk in the woods.
- Have a long talk with your spouse or a close friend.
- Sit in a different part of the worship area.
- Play with your children.
- See a movie with your team.

As a creative leader, I don't worry about dry spells. Instead, I tend to my spiritual life and encourage those around me to tend to theirs. My prayer is for our teams to stay passionately and powerfully close to God, and then give ourselves permission to dream big dreams on the foundation of that intimate relationship.

OVERCOMING OBSTACLES

When you work together as a team for a long time, you begin to realize that you've collectively learned a *lot* from the school of hard knocks. The following learnings have turned into valuable life lessons that we apply to other areas of our lives as well:

- Never say no to a good idea.
- Twenty-four hours is *plenty* of turnaround time.
- The speed of the players will adjust to the speed of the leaders.
- You're only leading if people are following.
- Good isn't nearly as much fun as great.
- Never save a great creative idea for later.
- You can't preach someone else's message.
- Discouragement wastes valuable time.

We've had more than our share of obstacles in worship design and ministry in general, but I am growing to believe that God's power is magnified through those very challenges. Our worst screwups are often the launching pads for God's best show-ups! Let me share a few examples.

The Scenario

It's the fall stewardship season. As a church, we'd realized that for postmodern Christians, tithing is no longer an unspoken assumption, and our offerings painfully revealed this discovery. We made a commitment to annually teach tithing and generous living in a strategic three-week stewardship series, culminating in a commitment weekend. (See Michael Slaughter with Kim Miller, *Money Matters: Financial Freedom for All God's Children* [Nashville: Abingdon Press, 2006].)

The Obstacle

Postmodern people don't know the definition of church words such as *stewardship* and *tithing*. We need to give information and inspiration without intimidation—all in thirty minutes! How do we teach these important lessons in a language that postmodern people can understand and receive?

The Overcoming

We're in our worship design meeting and have gotten as far as *nowhere*. How do we creatively inspire people toward lifestyles of generosity? One person happened to note that the concept of the tithe (10 percent) was most real to us as a culture within the context of the game of Monopoly.

> *My frequent prayer is for all creative teams to stay passionately and powerfully close to God, and then give ourselves permission to dream big dreams on the foundation of that intimate relationship.*

"Oh, you mean where the card says to pay 10 percent income tax?"

"Yeah, that's my only paradigm for the 10 percent rule."

"But that's about taxes, not tithing."

"So . . . what if . . . we came up with our *own* game?"

"What? Like Monopoly for Dummies?"

"Well, sort of, but we would have to make it our *own* and not be condescending."

"We could write a drama script about people playing Monopoly. That way we could use play money on the screen [in the main graphic] and avoid the stigma of real money!"

"Yeah, and the players could land on certain squares and have to pay a tithe. Then we could explain what a tithe is through the skit dialogue!"

"Oooh . . . we're getting somewhere. Then people won't feel so out of it, knowing that the lovable guy in the skit didn't know either."

"Now we're really getting somewhere."

"So what do we call it—the game—the weekend I mean?"

"I don't know; we can't call it Monopoly."

"True. How about Generous-opoly?"

"Generous-opoly . . . gener . . . opoly! *Generopoly*! The Game of Generous Living!"

"I love it; I love it; I love it!"

"Me too! I can't wait to write the script!"

We overcame the obstacle of the typical, dry stewardship sermon using language that people do not understand, by giving this celebration our best creative energies. You can read the results in the appendix. The Generopoly skit was terrific, and God showed up! Our annual stewardship series is now a favorite among our people and is never, *ever* boring! We are learning to understand how giving is a vital part of our transformation in Jesus. We continue to present ancient truths in culturally relevant ways, and God is glorified. Here's another example:

The Scenario

We have traditionally used the Dr. Martin Luther King, Jr., holiday weekend to deliver a message that reaffirms our call to demonstrate a multiracial and multigenerational kingdom community. Often we've invited a dynamic black preacher to deliver this important message that is always well received.

The Obstacle

On this particular MLK weekend, we needed an appropriate speaker but were having trouble finding one. We had thought that Mike would be in town and that he could use this message to recast his multicultural vision, but as it turned out, Mike had to be out of town.

The Overcoming

God had been working in the life of Francis Wyatt, our music director at that time, and I knew he had something to say. In addition, Fran was already part of the design team. He knew what it would take to present a powerful message to several thousand listeners. Most of Fran's real-life experiences growing up as an African American in St. Louis, Missouri, had yet to be told to our mostly white congregation. *Speaking on this weekend could only make Fran's worship-leading ministry more effective*, I thought.

And so Fran agreed to preach that weekend. We filled out the celebration with gospel songs and quotations from Dr. Martin Luther King, Jr. The rest of the team rallied around Fran in a huge way. His humble acceptance of our coaching, combined with the remarkable experiences he had to share, enabled him to preach a great message. In the end, Dayton's channel 22 news featured Ginghamsburg as its top story that night, amazed that a church in Tipp City (98 percent white community) would have such a multi-  cultural flavor of music. We overcame the obstacle, the absence of a "traditional" speaker, and God showed up in a powerful way.

The Scenario

Early one spring morning, Mike came excitedly into a design team meeting and told us the recent story about his sister's cat, which had been a stray at her door and wouldn't let up. Eventually, his sister "let the cat in," but only into one room of the house. Ultimately, after much persistence on the part of Socks, he was allowed free access to the entire house and has since become a beloved pet. "Socks is Jesus," Mike metaphorically explained. "Cool," we all responded. "What do we do with that?" After Mike left the room, someone spoke up, "We could give it a Dr. Seuss look a la *The Cat in the Hat!*"

The Obstacle

Dr. Seuss is not widely known as a source of *spiritual* inspiration. How would we take such a childish look and make it deeply spiritual? (Rule #1: We don't do *cute* at Ginghamsburg!) I wasn't sure how we'd accomplish it, but I challenged the team to "trust forward" that we'd figure it out.

The Overcoming

Our videographer went to Cincinnati to shoot the story featuring the real Socks. It would be a video at the beginning of Mike's message. (See the story of Socks on the Redesigning Worship Companion DVD.) Our graphic artist went to work on pictures with the help of a talented freehand artist. I secured a copy of the *The Cat in the Hat* from the library and began to dream: "What if I wrote a story so that Jesus shines through somehow?" I began to write a "storytelling" instead of a normal call to worship, featuring a young teacher telling the "Socks Knocks" story to real children sitting on real mats on the stage. The grown-ups in worship that weekend could see our re-created Seuss-like pictures on the screen as the storyteller turned the pages of her book.

I've included the resulting story in the appendix. "Socks Knocks"

became one of our most amazingly creative, spiritual, *and* appreciated weekends ever. People were touched by the familiarity of the Dr. Seuss look and the simplicity of Jesus' timeless invitation, "Behold, I stand at the door and knock" (Revelation 3:20). Our music leader then connected the message to the song celebration by reminding the congregation that "we've come to worship the One who calls to us, the One who is Savior and Lord."

Rather than miss out on a great, culturally familiar metaphor, we overcame the obstacle and instead *connected* the look to the Jesus story, and God showed up! At least a hundred people made first-time decisions to open the door of their hearts that weekend. (When was the last time you came forward to an altar only to find a swimming goldfish, a black umbrella, and a red-and-white-striped tall hat, all nicely arranged there?)

WHAT IS IN YOUR HAND?

Obstacles are nothing new. All the biblical movers and shakers had them. Our challenge is to move over, around, or directly through them as God leads. At first, Moses saw only obstacles to the mission. When he tried to look ahead, he saw only his low self-esteem, lack of the right social connections, and fear that the Israelites wouldn't believe that God had sent him.

But God is the ultimate overcomer, who stands poised and ready with resources to help us past the obstacles. In Exodus 4:2, God asked Moses the powerful question: "What is that in your hand?" I like that question.

What is in your hand? What do you *already have* that is familiar to you? It's your tool of the trade; it's your long suit; it's your strength; it's your best thing. What is in your hand? *Play to your strengths.* Just as God turned Moses' familiar walking stick into a powerful snake when Moses threw it down, God wants to take our best things, the most familiar tools from our hands, and make them more powerful for kingdom use.

I remember one stormy January Sunday morning at Ginghamsburg. Snow had been falling, blowing, and drifting for days. Our county was under a level three snow emergency, yet we were determined to have church for anyone who needed hope for his or her life. (No snow days for *us!*) The obstacle that day was clear: the storm would keep most of our musicians and media personnel at home because they lived some distance away.

What was in our hand? Mike was there and excited about delivering a teaching to a smaller group; that's what was in his hand. I could lead worship and play keyboards (not really well, but I *could*, and that's what was in my hand). Our graphic artist could play guitar in the absence of our regular musicians; that's what was in his hand. We pulled an image of a frost-covered mountain off the Internet to use as "stained-glass window" wallpaper on the screen. We sang, worshiped, prayed, and listened that day to what God wanted to say in the middle of the storm, and God showed up! All God asked us to do was to be faithful with what he'd already put in our hands.

What has God put in your hand? A beautiful old sanctuary? A unique urban setting for your ministry? A powerful storyteller? A donated cappuccino machine that's just begging to supply coffee to seekers in your lobby? Look in your hand, then trust God to begin to work with what you find there. Know you can overcome the obstacles that seem to be in your way. Keep moving forward, and don't be surprised when you discover that God has shown up!

CHAPTER 14

FOUR MANTRAS FOR THE MISSION

I thank God for my handicaps,
for, through them, I have found
myself, my work, and my God
— *Helen Keller*

When Jesus walked the earth, I'm sure he had his share of really bad days. Days when his team really didn't "get it." Days when he couldn't get enough time with his Boss. Days when the needs around him exceeded the resources available to do anything about them. Days when he might have wished he could call it quits.

I remember having one of those really bad days years ago. The team wasn't getting it. I couldn't seem to connect adequately with my coworkers, and it seemed that my problems outweighed my solutions ten to one. Knowing of my discouragement, Mike trudged into my office just before leaving for home and blurted out four action steps created on the spur of the moment for me. Four mantras, if you will. I wrote them on a yellow sticky note. Mike doesn't even remember saying them (which proves his hunch about how much he has in common with Balaam's donkey; he's just an available body for God to speak through!). But that little yellow square has been taped next to my computer ever since that day. Those mantras have guided me out of many dark moments. I hope they'll help you too.

MANTRA I: WORK IN THE PACKAGE GOD HAS GIVEN YOU

I praise you because I am fearfully and wonderfully made.
—King David, Psalm 139:14a

How many of us, after returning from a worship conference, find ourselves somewhat inspired, yet quietly confused? We've seen how others are doing it. We've observed their talent and the great ways that God is using them. We've written down everything the speaker had to say. We've made real decisions to do things better. Yet even in the wake of this wave of inspiration, we experience a disconnection: How am I supposed to replicate what they're doing? How is *our* church going to take all the necessary steps to become like *their* church?

Part of the good news of the gospel is that we don't have to try to be like anyone else. To attempt to replicate another worship leader's persona or ministry would be a slap in the face to the One who has "fearfully and wonderfully" made each one of us. Our creator God has given each one of us a unique package, a soul. Your soul is the unique part of you. Your soul is your personality, your God-given wiring, the you inside, the person you were created to be. *The Message* translates it this way:

Whoever did want him,
who believed he was who he claimed
and would do what he said,
He made to be their true selves,
their child-of-God selves.
—John 1:12

God esteem. We need it to thrive. The Bible commands us to love God with all of our minds, strength, hearts, and souls (Mark 12:30). We can't love God with our souls (much less teach others to do the

REDESIGNING WORSHIP

same) if we don't know who we are on the inside. When we strive to become someone else (even someone we admire), it's as if we've disowned our souls somewhere along the way. We can't become our true selves when we're trying to become someone else.

I need the community around me to keep reminding me of who I am in God. In my moments of discouragement, I've been known to sit myself down in front of my husband or a close friend and say, "Tell me again how God has equipped me for this job. I forget! Tell me again what you see God doing through me." I do forget, and hearing those kindred spirits tell me who I am in God's eyes refreshes me. It restores my soul. I have to *like me* before I can *love you.* Jesus said so: "Love the Lord your God," and "Love your neighbor as yourself" (Matthew 22:37, 39). I can't love God or others until I've embraced the gift of my soul, the unique part of me that God created, loves, and desires to work through.

God has given *you* a package, a soul. It's a gift to use as you live out your God dreams. It's your gift to exercise as you design worship experiences that will draw others to know that same kind of grace and acceptance from God.

Once while designing a worship experience that I hoped would guide participants to truly understand and embrace this amazing-grace kind of love, I rewrote Psalm 23 as though I was speaking it to God in my own words. I asked the members of the congregation to close their eyes as they imagined this intimate interchange with God:

THE LORD IS MY SHEPHERD

The Lord is my shepherd—mine, all mine. He remembers to feed me. He presses oil into my wounds. He counts me as his own, for I am important to him. When I'm missing, he comes after me. He won't sleep if I can't. He loves me and I shall not want. There's nothing I could need that he hasn't assessed and blessed on me.

This God makes me lie down in green pastures. And I'm just gonna lie here and stare at the sky and dream. Dream about what can be now that the sky's the limit. Dream about my kids, my family, my friends, and all God will do in their lives . . . just because I asked and God can.

This God leads me beside still waters. I look down at my reflection—I can see it clearly. I am the son, the daughter, the beloved child of the most high God . . . and I like being that person. God has taught me that love.

This God, my Shepherd, restores my soul. Perfect? No. Lovable? Yes. Restoration can be appreciated only by the sinful, the broken, the spiritually challenged . . . the shamed child, the abused teen, the overwhelmed mother or father.

This God restores my soul, picks me up, and leads me on a new path of righteousness, not for my sake or my glory, but for his name's sake. Yes, I will walk through the valley of the shadow of death. We all will, but we will fear no evil. Evil cannot touch us. The shadow of death is simply a shadow—not the real deal. For you are with me.

Death, where is your sting? Grave, you have no victory. Jesus the Shepherd is here. His rod of fierce protection, his staff of clear direction, they comfort me.

You prepare a table before me in the presence of my enemies. You've written my name on the invitation; you've anointed my head with oil . . .

You've deemed me forgiven and useful for service. Those who rejected you now watch while you and I eat and laugh and talk together. I keep drinking out of my cup, but it keeps getting refilled to overflowing. You're amazing, God. Surely this God's goodness and mercy—the unconditional, unrelenting, unbridled love of God—shall be with us all of our lives. Every day if we will only look for it . . . if our ears will simply listen . . . if our hearts will readily receive it. And we will live in God's house forever. Amen.

As worship designers, we must work in the package God has given us. How is God best able to use you and your team? What is the language you speak best? Some people are oral communicators, masters of the spoken word. Others say it best with pictures, carefully aiming the camera at the most important thing. Some are careful planners, making each moment count, using people and resources to their fullest potential. Others gifted in relationship building can communicate by their congregational connectivity. God will use them to make others feel welcomed and loved.

Each one of us absolutely must work in the package God has given us. While some are best one-on-one, I am better in front of a crowd. While some can paint beautiful pictures with a brush, my best art is in the arrangement of tactile objects. Some people are powerfully gifted vocalists who minister through song. I'm better at interweaving popular songs with biblical storytelling and choosing just the right people to sing and speak them. That is my package, and I'm learning to be comfortable in it.

MANTRA 2: TELL THE TRUTH

When Jesus boldly announced, "The truth shall set you free," was he referring to the truth about God or the truth about everything? Could this statement have been a piece of wisdom that Jesus believed, demonstrated, and lived out every single day of his life? I believe Jesus was stating that the truth, any truth about any given life situation, would ultimately set us free if we could but discover it and speak it.

Telling the truth to one another in community is nothing short of an art form. We speak the truth in order to build up one another, to give constructive insight into one another's life stories. (This is not an invitation to blanket our coworkers with criticism or announce our personal opinions to the world!) As we tell the truth within our teams, we must be motivated by love. We must hope for and intend success for everyone involved. We must join in one desire to enjoy all God's best gifts as a team, a community, and a church.

As worship team leaders, we hold the stewardship of the congregation's worship experience. Our job is to consistently and continually tell the truth about our worship pieces so that the pieces might best serve the kingdom. In the best sense of truth telling, this means affirmation whenever possible, and suggestions for improvement when improvement is called for.

Our team has made it a practice to tell one another the truth as much as possible. I tell Mike the truth about his messages and how they affect me. I tell our music leaders the truth about their growth as lead worshipers and how the music has affected my worship on any given weekend. We tell our media producers the truth about how their pieces affect us, styles that engage us and where they could connect with people a bit better. I ask others to tell me the truth about pieces I have prepared as well: "Did that connect? What do you think about this storytelling script? How does the stage look to you? Do you think we're on target here?"

Being truthful is imperative for our growth process. I remember a time early on when as an unpaid servant, I had pulled together and coached a team of four women to execute a drama using a purchased script I'd found in a catalog. These women were doing an excellent job of acting. I had created the drama set, and we had rehearsed and performed the drama for our Saturday night celebration. Afterward as the worship team debriefed together, Mike told me the truth as he saw it: "The drama is good, Kim, but it doesn't really go with the message. There's a disconnection for me. I'd recommend we pull it from tomorrow's worship celebrations."

That was devastating news, of course, since we'd obviously put in a significant amount of time and work. I reluctantly agreed to drop the drama, but in responding I told the truth about my feelings. "I feel bad about this for myself and mostly for the others involved," I replied, "but I'll do the best thing for the church family and the overall worship experience."

I went home, prayed for strength and courage, and then phoned each of the four actors. "You did an awesome job tonight, and I loved working with you," I told each one, "but in the end, the drama did not connect with the sermon the way we'd hoped for. It isn't anyone's fault. We would love to use the drama and especially your gifts in the future, but we're going to have to pull it from tomorrow's celebrations."

While I told the truth, I affirmed each person's contribution. Much to my amazement, not one of them reacted negatively, and each one has had opportunities to serve in dramatic roles since that time. The worship celebrations the next morning were much better, the word was much more powerful without the confusing drama, and God was honored.

The simple truth set us all free, and I grew in the process. Here is what I learned that weekend that has stuck with me—freedom lessons I've since used again and again:

- No matter how great a drama is, it cannot play a powerful role in the worship celebration without a direct connection to the message.
- The majority of our dramatic scripts need to be original and written by someone who knows and understands the intention of the speaker's message.
- Most people can handle the truth if it's spoken with love and authenticity, affirming the things they've done well.
- The way we react in times of great challenge or seeming opposition reveals our true character.
- Others on the team can trust me with their true feelings.

When I tell the truth, other team members are freed to do the same. All that makes the next mantra a more viable possibility . . .

MANTRA 3: DO THE RIGHT THING, NOT THE EXPECTED THING

Author Anne Lamott wrote, "Hope begins in the dark, the stubborn hope that if you just show up and try to do the right thing, the dawn will come. You wait and watch and work: you don't give up" (*Bird by Bird*, New York: Anchor Books, 1995).

Powerful God experiences are not going to spontaneously descend into your worship space. This is not to say that God won't powerfully "show up" unannounced at various times, but that God has always honored the work of those who pray, prepare, and persevere in doing the right things rather than choose the easy way out. We may be tempted to take the easy path in several ways:

- By allowing team players to come and go from a design team meeting as they wish, never bringing focus to the worship planning process.
- By using the same tried-and-true worship songs rather than searching for new possibilities. Remember, God wants us to "sing to him a new song" (Psalm 33:3).
- By saying, "That's not my job," when faced with a task we don't want to take on.

Even as I write this list, I am aware that this mantra permeates absolutely everything we do here at Ginghamsburg—the list could go on and on! This is a piece of our team's DNA that we cannot minimize or overlook. We know we will never make our best decisions unless we set aside our fears of encountering resistance or increasing our workloads. We recognize that if we try, we may fail. But most of the time we try anyway. If we want our worship dreams to succeed, we know that we must wake up every day and do the hard things, the right things.

Most people want to live incredible lives. Most worship designers want to encourage powerful God experiences, but we tend to underestimate all it will take to get there. Thomas Edison said, "Genius is one percent inspiration, ninety-nine percent perspiration." Jesus Christ said, "Small is the gate and narrow the road that leads to life, and only a few find it" (Matthew 7:14). There are no shortcuts to this endeavor. It's a thousand little decisions every single week. When we've chosen to live life on the narrow way, we must work hard to maximize every single moment of the worship experience. Thankfully, Jesus will never leave us alone on the path.

MANTRA 4: GO IN GOD'S AUTHORITY

You will receive power when the Holy Spirit comes on you. —Luke, Acts 1:8a

Moses was obviously chosen by God for one of the most monumental leadership tasks of the entire Old Testament. An Israelite by birth, Moses had been raised as an Egyptian. He had the perfect crossover credentials to succeed in delivering God's chosen people from slavery. The only trouble with Moses was inside Moses himself. He didn't realize how uniquely gifted he was, nor did he recognize the power of God being offered to him in the deal. Moses was full of excuses for why he couldn't pull off the Promised Land Proposal.

I've had my own set of excuses. I've even spiritualized them at times . . . excuses about why God could use others much more effectively. Here's my short list. (I'll spare you the long one.)

- I'm a female (and grew up in a denomination that refused to recognize females as leadership material).
- I'm a *small* female (easy to be underestimated).
- I didn't pursue a four-year college degree.
- I'm not particularly left-brained, and my right-brained tendencies can be very limiting in certain structured scenarios.
- My dad was mentally ill, creating a dysfunctional childhood environment.
- I'm not ordained clergy.

How's that for starters? How ironic that I would be signed up to serve as creative director, giving leadership in a megachurch whose empowerment theology has challenged every one of my excuses. My challenge to go in God's authority has increased as I've occasionally been called on to create powerful God experiences without a preacher; I've even had to *be* the preacher on occasion.

For me, "go in God's authority" usually translates as "feel the fear and do it anyway." God will do the rest. God's question to Moses, "What is that in your hand?" is a question for me as well. God works in me, just as God worked in Moses, to convince me to rely on divine authority rather than my own. "In my hand," I know I can count on a passionate band, versatile vocalists, motivated media-savvy partners, and a team who will put up with and build our collective wildest worship dreams. Also in my hand is my creative ability to pull all kinds of diverse, multimedia pieces together to produce a cohesive and powerful message.

As a team, we've had to ask, "What is in our hand?" as we've encountered occasional weekends when we dream, develop, and deploy worship together without the aid of a preacher. We refer to these experiences as "team weeks." On these weeks the leader (me or another player) comes with a word, a theme, and a core truth, and the team then creates a worship experience with music, drama, and media—but no traditional sermon or message.

Our first team week fell on a pre-Thanksgiving weekend a few years back. With no traditional message giver on the schedule, we knew as a team that we'd be the messengers for the weekend . . . that we must move out and *go in God's authority*. As we met to design the worship celebration, we agreed on a few key things:

- The bulk of the message time could and should be God stories—video or live testimonies of God at work in our people's lives.
- This pre-Thanksgiving worship celebration should not just remind participants to be thankful. Rather, it should encourage them to rejoice *in the midst* of painful situations.
- The celebrations must include a word of hope, for "we know that in all things God works for the good of those who love him, who have been called according to his purpose" (Romans 8:28). This scripture helped give form to our creative work.

We asked additional staffers to join us in room 202 to help brainstorm a list of the possible God stories we could feature. Some of our favorites came from people inside that room. One staff person's unmarried daughter had just announced an unexpected pregnancy.

Several years ago, another person's baby had died of complications at just three months of age. A third story would describe the experience of a fifty-something-aged couple, husband and wife, both Ginghamsburg servants, battling the wife's cancer.

As we contemplated the potential of telling these family stories with the larger congregation, an idea came up that unlocked our creativity: "We can frame this around the dance of life! 'We Danced Anyway' is a great song I've been wanting to do."

Immediately, the team knew we were onto something powerful, an alternative Thanksgiving celebration—three stories about God's faithfulness in the midst of challenging life circumstances. Two of these stories were told digitally, and another was presented as a live monologue (it is included in the worship script provided in the appendix). You may want to use this script outline and insert stories from your church community.

we danced anyway

We have challenged our congregation to *go in God's authority* by telling their stories to encourage others. It's exciting to see how real people have responded with real stories that become part of God's movement to do real kingdom work. One of our church's principles of renewal is the Priesthood Principle. (See Michael Slaughter, *Spiritual Entrepreneurs* [Nashville: Abingdon Press, 1995].) Simply put, this principle states that God works best through everyday people. Ginghamsburg is a movement not of professional clergy, but of everyday, ordinary people, real followers committed to carry out the mission of Jesus on planet earth. Postmodern worship is a lot about storytelling, and the more people are empowered to *go in God's authority*, the more stories there will be to tell.

On a more recent Palm Sunday weekend, we invited a larger group of unpaid servants to join us for a team week. "In our hand" was a story, the story of Jesus' last week on earth. As a church, we had not chronicled that story together in worship for at least ten years. I began mapping out a musical drama, keeping in mind the strengths of the people who might be part of such an event. As we endeavored to move ahead in God's authority, we were again met by a powerful God experience. Many from our congregation remarked afterward that it was their favorite worship celebration ever. (You'll find an outline of that worship experience in the appendix.)

THE MESSAGE OF THE MANTRAS

All four of these mantras have guided me as I've worked with people, projects, and God possibilities. Remembering them has been so *freeing* as I make daily decisions that will have eternal impact. Whether casting roles for a children's musical or designing a special altar for a 9/11 anniversary, I hear God say, "Kim, just work inside of who you are; tell the truth! Do the right thing, not the expected thing. I have given you all authority—for heaven's sake . . . go!"

Ignoring these four mantras, we find that we have music without passion, media without power, and messages without purpose. I don't know anyone who wants to be part of a mediocre movement. We don't want to meet our Maker only to find out what God *could* have done through our lives if we hadn't played it safe and done the comfortable thing rather than risked doing the creative thing.

It's amazing to see what kinds of miracles unfold when we *work in the unique packages God has given us*; when we *speak the truth in love*; when we determine to *do what is right, not merely what's expected*; and when we step out and *go in God's authority*. By exercising these mantras, ordinary people will demonstrate the power of an extraordinary God!

SEND OUT:
A MINISTRY OF MUD 'N' SPIT

What does it take to make a miracle happen?

In our limited perspectives, we fancy God with sparkling magic potions carefully arranged in a glittering heavenly toolbox. Maybe a few wands thrown in for the really tough jobs.

God's best work, however, has always been done with amazingly ordinary stuff—water, mud, spit, a piece of stale bread, a barn, a teenaged girl, twelve dysfunctional disciples. Ordinary objects in regular places with everyday people. The good news for every single worship designer on the planet is that miracles happen when the Divine intersects with the ordinary.

I am but one woman with a very alternative education. I think way too many thoughts and have a passion for Jesus and the church. I'm not a very big person, and I still get knots in my stomach every time we unveil a newly designed environment, a trendy office makeover, or an innovative worship experience; but look out when I set my mind to something.

The metaphor I use for my life is "mud and spit." I'm fascinated with the four Gospels and the earthiness of everything Jesus did. I'm not sure if it had been in this millennium how Jesus would've healed the blind man in the Gospel of John, chapter 9. Maybe he would've used some thick espresso or some aromatic candle wax. On that particular day, however, Jesus spat in the dust, making a clay paste with his saliva, and rubbed that paste onto the blind man's eyes—then told him to wash in a certain pool. That's creativity. That's using what you have, where you have it, and whom you have it with—I love that! Stories like that give me hope that I can do this too. I'm an everyday person. I've been touched by heaven, empowered by God. I can use what God has already put in me and around me, just ordinary stuff, and begin to change the world.

Ours is a ministry of mud and spit. God wants each and every one of us to know that with God's spirit, we are uniquely gifted to be a part of making miracles happen. Everyday people using ordinary objects in regular places to create powerful God experiences. And as I bring this writing to a close, here is your very first assignment for redesigning worship, straight from a little yellow sticky note next to my computer:

- Care more than others think wise.
- Risk more than others think safe.
- Dream more than others think practical.
- Expect more than others think possible.

Amen.

SAMPLE SCRIPTS FOR WORSHIP CELEBRATIONS

GREAT EXPECTATIONS

an Advent storytelling

Biblical Story: Zechariah's Dilemma (adapted from Luke 1:5-24)
Actors: One storyteller (Story can be read from a script.)
Costume: None
Sct: None
Suggested Song: "I Can't Fight This Feeling Anymore" (REO Speedwagon) (It is not necessary to obtain permission to use this music if it's performed live in a worship celebration.)
Description: Storyteller is seated on stage, lit separately from the band if possible. On-screen, show hand-drawn or scanned illustrations of the Bible story. After the storyteller finishes each section, resume the song.

Perform the first verse of the song vocally, then play a soft, instrumental version under the storytelling.

STORYTELLER: During the rule of Herod, king of Judea, there was a priest in the regiment of Abijah whose name was Zechariah. His wife was named Elizabeth. Together they lived honorably before God, careful to keep the commandments and enjoying a clear conscience before God, but they were childless because Elizabeth could never conceive, and now they were quite old.

It so happened that while Zechariah was carrying out his priestly duties before God, he was chosen to enter the sanctuary of God and burn incense. The congregation was gathered and praying outside the temple at that hour. Unannounced, an angel of God appeared next to the altar of incense. Zechariah was paralyzed in fear. But the angel assured him, "Your prayer has been heard. Elizabeth, your wife, will bear a son by you. You are to name him John."

Sing the second verse of the song, then play soft, instrumental music under the storytelling.

STORYTELLER: "You're going to leap for joy, Zechariah," the angel spoke, "and not only you, but many will delight in John's birth. He'll achieve great stature with God. He'll be filled with the Holy Spirit from the moment he's born. He will turn many sons and daughters of Israel back to their God. He will herald God's arrival in the style and strength of Elijah, soften the hearts of parents to children, and kindle understanding among hardened skeptics; he'll get the people ready for the Messiah."

Sing the song's third and fourth verses, then play soft, instrumental music under the storytelling.

STORYTELLER: Zechariah said to the angel, "Do you expect me to believe this? I'm an old man and my wife is an old woman." But the angel said, "I am Gabriel, sent by God, sent especially to bring you this news. But because you won't believe, you'll be unable to speak a word until the day of your son's birth. Every word I've spoken to you will come true on time . . . God's time."

Meanwhile, the congregation waiting for Zechariah was getting restless, wondering what was keeping him so long in the sanctuary. When he came out and couldn't speak, they knew he had seen a vision. Zechariah continued speechless and had to use sign language with the people.

When the course of his priestly assignment was completed, Zechariah went back home. It wasn't long before his wife, Elizabeth, conceived.

Resume song and play to the end.

REDESIGNING WORSHIP

AIM HIGH

finding strength and confidence in God

Biblical Story: David (from 1 Samuel 16:1-17)
Actors: Two males, one age ten to thirteen and one age twenty to thirty. Their appearances should be similar enough to convey a younger and older version of a single individual.
Costume: Both males wear identical costumes: jeans with holes, a white T-shirt, and the same bandana. Both are barefoot and have slingshots with a rock.
Set: Large rock(s) to give the ambience of a shepherd's space
Suggested Song: "Man After Your Own Heart" (Wayne Kirkpatrick and Billy Sprague, performed by Gary Chapman) (Music must be obtained separately.)
Description: This is a two-part drama. The first monologue begins during the instrumental introduction. The younger David is seated on a rock. He begins talking as the lights go up. He is confident and passionate. As the vocalist sings two verses, the older David approaches the set. He walks slowly, and the two Davids pass each other as the younger David leaves the stage. The older David delivers his monologue, then exits after the lights go dark. After he leaves, the vocalist finishes the song.

At the designated points in the song, pause the vocals, and have the actors deliver their monologues. Continue to play soft instrumental music under the actors' spoken words. After each monologue, resume the song.

MONOLOGUE 1 (Younger David)

A young boy is seated on a rock. He is a bit cocky and outspoken and is fooling around with a slingshot. He begins talking as lights go up. *(Lights up)*

Play the instrumental introduction. Monologue 1 is spoken over music.

YOUNGER DAVID: Hi. My name's Davey. Nobody really calls me David much . . .'cept my old man . . . when he's mad.

(Getting more excited) Have you ever shot a rock from a slingshot? I have. *(Standing)* I could hit that light up there *(pointing up)* and break it in a million pieces. I could nail one right between your eyes . . . if I ever needed to, which I don't. *(Sits back down)*

Mostly what I do is kill animals. My dad owns some sheep, and they couldn't defend themselves if their lives depended on it, which they do.

So I go after the lions and the bears. *(Looking at the audience)* You don't believe me, but I do. When you're out in the hills, you get a lot of time to practice. Here's what I say every time I'm up against a bear. *(Standing)* "God, I love you with everything I have, and today there is nothing we can't do together." And then I just go for it . . . aim high. *(Lights blackout)*

Continue the song through the first two verses as older David approaches. Then play soft, instrumental music under monologue.

MONOLOGUE 2 (Older David)

A young man is seated on a rock. His personality is confident and passionate. He holds a slingshot. He begins talking as the lights go up. *(Lights up as David begins to speak)*

OLDER DAVID: Name's David. You might know me for a lot of things, but I need to tell you firsthand what happened with the "Goliath Project."

I was always the "runt of the litter," as you would say. The youngest of eight sons of my old man, Jesse. I don't have to tell you I got the bad end of everything. The older ones always got the best jobs while I was left looking after our sorry little sheep. They got to go fight when I stayed back.

But it wasn't all bad. I learned about the companionship of God—yep, God. Ever since I was young, I've been preoccupied with the unseen Presence. It was God who taught me to just stand and aim high. I'm a straight shot with a reckless passion. Cocky, too. I'd learned to hunt down lions and bears. But after a while I found myself going after the heart of my God.

Oh, and I am a little crazy, too. So when I catch a look at this jerk, Goliath, who dares to defy the army of my God, I tell them all that it's going to be OK. It's God's battle, and I can nail this guy right between the eyes. Well, God and I. Yeah. Aim high. *(Lights blackout; older David exits)*

Resume song and play to the end.

EVERY DAY

a reader's theater about New Year's resolutions

Theme: Devotion to God

Actors: Three readers, ages eighteen to twenty-eight (Try to vary gender and race.)

Costume: Casual dress in appropriate Gen-X style

Set: Three stools that can be lit separately from the band

Song: "Everyday" (Dave Matthews Band) (Music must be obtained separately.)

Description: Reader's theater with three readers. Reader one is a skeptical resolution maker, reader two is overly optimistic and materialistic, and reader three is more tuned in to devotion to God. All are oblivious of one another. When saying their lines, it appears that each is making a list of new year's resolutions, equipped with a notebook and pen.

As each reader finishes his or her line, the next reader says the same word at the same time to lead into his or her next line. Overlapping words are indicated by italics in the script. The entire piece is spoken in two "pockets" at appropriate breaks in the Dave Matthews song "Everyday." Breaks should be timed at the discretion of the band leader, with instrumental music continuing softly under the readers.

Begin the song. When the band leader breaks, begin the following dialogue.

READER 1: Let's see . . . January 201_. I can't believe it. Better put down some resolutions before this year gets away from me. *Number one* . . .

READER 2: *Number one* . . . lose ten pounds. That's how much I think I gained over *Christmas.*

READER 1: *Christmas* was so fattening! I better start exercising! I hate to think about it, but hey, no time like the *present.*

READER 3: *Presence.* I need the presence of God in my life every day. Here I am, Lord. I'm not gonna let go of you *this year.*

READER 1: *This year* should be the year for my new job. I hate just going through the motions week in and week out. I hereby make a resolution to find something I can really sink my teeth into *every day*.

READER 3: *Every day* will be a new day with you, Jesus. Part of not letting go of you is my promise to be more honest with you. I need someone who can listen to everything, who understands *my struggles*.

READER 2: *My struggle* is with that old piece of junk I'm driving. A car. This is the year of the car! I'm thinking the new Audi TT! *Yes!*

READER 3: *Yes!* Because, Jesus, if I can't be totally real with you, well, what good is our relationship? And I want to know the real "you."

Resume music. Break at band leader's discretion. Readers continue.

READER 2: Blue. My new car will be blue. This is gonna be a great *year!*

READER 1: *Years* come and go. I'm twenty-three, for heaven's sake. I'm going to finally map out that five-year plan that my dad always told me I needed. Should that be a today thing? *O Lord . . .*

READER 3: *O Lord*, if I spend time with you every day, would I . . . do you think I could "hear" from you? Do you give directions to people? Plans? Ideas? *Dreams?*

READER 2: *Dreams* are what life is made of. I'm dreaming of a green new year (if you know what *I mean*).

READER 1: *I mean*, it's crazy to think I can keep my resolutions. It's never happened before! Even if I do apply for a better job, there's no guarantee I would be able to *get it*.

READER 3: *Get it!* I get it! I'll meet you here, Lord, *every day!*

READER 2: *Every day* I'm gonna go for it. The car, the dream, the money *every day*.

READER 1: *Every day*. O Lord, I can't believe I'll have to pull my life together again every single morning.

ALL: Every day!

GENEROPOLY

the game of generous giving

Actors: Two young men and two young women

Costume: Casual dress

Set: A game table and four chairs. On the table is a game of Generopoly, four bottles of soda, and any other props appropriate to game night.

Description: The band begins by singing "If I Had a Million Dollars." Two young men and two young women approach the stage, talking and laughing in muted tones, then settle in on the set at the table. (*Low lights up on drama.*) The players continue to set up the game, occasionally singing along with the band.

The band finishes the song. (Lights up on drama, down on band)

B.J.: (*to band*) We'll take it from here, guys. If I had a million dollars . . .

TERRI: If I had a million dollars . . .

CARL: No, if I had a million dollars . . .

ABBY: What? What would you do with it?

CARL: Well, let's just say I wouldn't be sitting here gearing up for another night of classic Monopoly.

ABBY: (*holding up the lid like Vanna White*) Not Monopoly, Carl, Generopoly—The Game of Generous Giving.

CARL: What's that about?

TERRI: It probably wouldn't hurt you to find out.

CARL: I can play that game—bring it on!

B.J.: Might not be as easy as you think, big guy.

ABBY: I think it depends on what kind of person you are . . .

TERRI: Take your turn—you're first.

CARL: OK, OK. (*He rolls and quickly moves to the space marked "Income Tithe," counting one-two-three-four*) Income Tax—no, wait—"Income Tithe. Pay 10 percent or $200.00." Can somebody tell me what "Income Tithe" is?

ABBY: Tithe means 10 percent. You give 10 percent of your income.

CARL: You mean just . . . give?

ABBY: Yeah . . . give. Give up, like to God. You give God 10 percent or so, and God takes care of everything else you need. Comprende?

CARL: (*sarcastically*) Oh, that's great.

B.J.: I don't get it.

TERRI: Well, it is Generopoly. See what the card says? "Seek first the kingdom of God and all the rest will be given to you."

CARL: So you're saying I could still win?

ABBY: Sure you could. Let's keep going, Terri.

TERRI: OK, sure. I'll just hop on down the neighborhood here . . . (*rolls and counts*) St. Charles Place . . . I'll take it! Sounds like a great street for a single-parent housing unit.

CARL: Single-parent housing unit . . . have I missed something here?

ABBY: Maybe that this game is about giving, not getting.

TERRI: That's always been a hard concept for Carl to grasp.

CARL: Hey!

TERRI: Sorry.

B.J.: (*rolling*) This is my lucky day . . . I can just feel it (*rolls and moves to Community Chest*). Oh, cool, Community Chest!

ABBY: Not Community Chest, B.J. Treasure Chest. It's called "Treasure Chest" in this game. Pick up the card.

B.J.: (*picking up the card*) Hmm . . . "You just opened a shelter for the homeless, and you'll need to buy food. Collect $150.00."

CARL: What?

B.J.: Hey, I'm getting it now. It's Generopoly! Read the fine print on the card: "For where your treasure is, there will your heart be also." I like this game!

CARL: It isn't making a lot of sense—it seems backward.

ABBY: My turn (*grabbing the dice*). I've got a great feeling here (*rolls, moves, and picks up card*). Chance: "Congratulations! You used your vacation to build a home at a project in Mississippi. Advance to the nearest railroad, and it's yours for your next trip."

CARL: This is ridiculous. I'm sitting here competing with Mother Teresa on the Reading Railroad, the pope's feeding the hungry, and the church lady here is putting up single-parent housing in place of red hotels. Give me those dice. (*He rolls and moves*) Treasure Chest. Hmm—maybe I'll get lucky, I need a break. (*He reads the card*) "When given the opportunity to sponsor a needy child at church, you kept the money and purchased five Big Macs instead. Go to jail. Go directly to jail. Do not pass Go . . ."

All: "Do not collect $200."

CARL: Thanks, everybody.

All: No problem! (*ad lib*)

CARL: Then again, maybe I do have a problem.

B.J.: Admitting it is always the first step toward recovery. What is the problem you speak of?

CARL: I can't seem to get this. It seems rigged or something. You can't get ahead in this game without giving something away. It's not natural for me—I don't think that way.

TERRI: But you should . . . (*Carl glares at her*) could! I mean, you could. You can learn generous giving.

ABBY: Terri's right. It's a whole different way of living.

B.J.: Think of it as making a Boardwalk salary . . . but choosing a Baltic Avenue lifestyle.

CARL: Oooh . . . that hurts.

TERRI: 'Cause no one can serve two masters.

ABBY: Even if he does have a million dollars!

(Lights blackout)

(Band reprises "If I Had a Million Dollars")

SOCKS KNOCKS

a call to worship story

A Call to Worship Story

The sun did not shine; it was too wet to play.
So we sat in the house all that cold, cold day.
I sat there with Susie; we sat there, we two.
And I said, "It looks to me like we've nothing to do."

Too wet to go out and too cold to play ball.
So we sat in the house; we did nothing at all.
So all that we did was sit! sit! sit! sit!
And we did not like it, not one little bit.

And then, something went bump!
How that bump made us jump!
We looked, then we saw him outside on the mat.
We looked and we saw him, this little black cat.

We looked at that cat mewing outside the door.
We knew Dad would say, "This cat is no more.
No more can this cat be inside of our house,
Than a dog or a bird or a horse or a mouse.

For cats are not good, and houses need locks.
And no one who lives here will answer their knocks."
Because even if cats are cute like a fox,
Even if cats have white feet just like Socks,

And even if cats call and ask to come in,
You just can't give up and feed them and then . . .
Wish that you hadn't, for Dad says, "You know . . .
That cat's too much trouble; that cat's got to go!"

Now why, you may ask, tell this tale here in church?
"Please," you are saying, "get us out of this lurch!"

For cats are not bad, and dads not all mean.
And so what is the point that remains to be seen?
I'll tell you now . . .
Jesus the Savior calls from outside the door,
"Listen to me, I'm asking for more.
I'm asking for you to let me come in,
To come live with you, to clean out the sin.

"I want to live now in this house here with you.
I want to share all of the things that you do."
Behold, the Lord Jesus stands there and knocks.
Not unlike the cat, whose name was called Socks.
But grown-ups, their lives full of sin! sin! sin! sin!
Can close themselves up, and not let him come in.

So today is a call to listen to him,
To open the door of your life full of sin,
To ask him to come in, and eat with you too,
'Cause life with this Jesus is all up to *you*!

WE DANCED ANYWAY

thankfulness in the midst of struggles

Word: "We know that in all things God works for the good of those who love him, who have been called according to his purpose" (Romans 8:28); 1 Thessalonians 5:18; Psalm 30

Felt Need: I don't understand how to "dance" (be thankful) when my world is falling apart.

Desired Outcome: Participants will choose to "dance" anyway, unleashing God's strength and power.

Theme: We Danced Anyway

Look: Ballet dancer

Play video clip from the movie Hope Floats *(scene that begins with Sandra Bullock speaking to her father, then they begin dancing).*

Begin live music while the characters in the video are dancing. Fade video clip and bring up live music (band and vocalist), "We Danced Anyway."

OPENING WORDS: Someone once said that life is what really happens on the way to your dreams. In other words, things don't always go as we plan them. . . . Parents grow old.

Relationships get broken.

Children go a different way.

Life can become painful, and you and I forget to dance.

Today is going to be a different kind of experience. There are great stories of faith in this room, and today we are going to teach one another about faith, about true thanksgiving, and about dancing through tough times. Today is the story of a God who calls us to give thanks no matter what happens . . .

even when it's not our plan,

even when it hurts,

even when it doesn't make sense, and even when we don't understand the words.

God invites us to dance anyway and teaches us the steps.

Today we hear the stories of real people who have felt the blow of real pain, who've cried a multitude of tears, and yet, through it all, have learned to dance anyway.

Today is your story too. Whatever is going on in each of our lives, we need to step out and begin to dance, saying, "Thank you, God. We trust you no matter what. And even though we don't always understand the words, we open ourselves to your presence and power in our lives, through our tears and in our pain. We dance anyway."

Play video or invite live speakers to share their stories. After the stories, the worship leader leads the congregation members in praying for each other as the band plays softly. At the end of the prayer time, continue with the worship celebration. Suggested additional songs include "I Need You" by LeAnn Rimes (to be sung as the offering is collected), "The Dance" by Garth Brooks, and "I Hope You Dance" by Lee Ann Womack.

Invite additional speakers to share their stories. The story we used at Ginghamsburg follows below. A keyboardist provides soft piano music in the background as the speaker tells his or her story.

SPEAKER: On May 25, 1995, we lost a child. Lydia was eighty-six days old when her heart stopped. We knew there were problems with her heart and were anticipating surgery to repair the abnormalities. She had just begun smiling and was fascinated with her hands. Although I knew she was ill, I was devastated when she was suddenly gone. How could I get through the day? Life changed instantly for us. Many people avoided us because they didn't know what to say. Others said the wrong things. The honest truth is there is little to say in the face of a tragedy like losing a child. Initially, nothing could replace our lost child, comfort our grief, or fill the hole in our hearts.

I want to wear a T-shirt that says, "Be nice to me; my child just died." I find myself short-tempered, humorless, and impatient . . . just dancing the dance. I went to a party, and a young couple was there with their firstborn, a beautiful, blue-eyed butterball. I found out her name was Lydia and she was born three weeks after my Lydia. Will I ever be able to look at her without seeing what my little girl could have been?

Dancing the dance. I bravely drove to the hospital where Lydia spent several weeks in intensive care. Though painful, I walked through the halls and the memories to visit a friend who had just given birth to her long-awaited daughter. I masked my tears and shared her joy . . . dancing the dance.

J. C. Penney sends me a Happy Birthday card announcing their photography studio specials for "LYDIA WHO'S ONE!" I'm surprised when I open the card, surprised that I didn't expect it, and surprised at my irrational hostility. I never want to buy anything at J.C. Penney again. Dancing the dance.

I sob like a baby, watching happy TV shows: sappy commercials, bad made-for-TV movies, Kathie Lee Gifford's stories about her kids. Life is so precious, and I'm grateful for each day that I have to share it with those that I love. Dancing the dance.

The dance of Lydia's life was painful because it ended much too soon. The dance of grief is one we're forced into, catching us off guard and sweeping us into its wretched rhythm. But if we're willing, God will join us there and comfort us. I find myself thinking about how different life would be if Lydia had never been here. "I could have missed the pain, but I'd have had to miss the dance."

Begin playing "The Dance." Pause or lower the music in the middle of the song so the audience can hear the speaker or worship leader read the following paraphrase of a passage from The Message.

SPEAKER: I will lift you up, God, because you lifted me out of the depths. There was a time when I screamed, "Good Lord, where are you?" Then you touched my despairing soul with healing and delivered me from my own private hell. All who believe, give your praise to God. The nights of crying your eyes out give way to days of laughter. When things were going great, I felt secure. You favored me, Lord. Then you looked the other way, and I fell to pieces. I called out to you, Lord, holding on to hope by my fingernails. I cried for mercy. If I'm dead and gone, how can I praise you? Hear me and be merciful to me. Help me. Help me to dance. Change my wailing into whirling dance. Remove my clothing of despair and replace it with a cloak of joy. Lord, I'm about to burst with song; I can't keep quiet about you. God, my God, I love you so much. I'll dance anyway.

Finish playing "The Dance." Then the worship leader leads the congregation in prayers for children or others. The band plays "I Hope You Dance."

Provide words on-screen or in print for the following responsive closing.

LEADER: With the living and eternal God as our goal and guide, fear and anxiety need have no place in our lives.

ALL: So we choose to dance anyway.

LEADER: All the evil in the world cannot destroy the Lord, nor can it destroy anyone within God's loving embrace.

ALL: So we choose to dance anyway.

LEADER: We stand tall, regardless of threatening enemies and the pain of evil.

ALL: So we choose to dance anyway.

LEADER: Our God hears when we cry out and will not ignore our needs. We dedicate ourselves anew to you, O Lord. We will serve you whatever the cost or the consequence. We will praise your name and proclaim your love to people all around.

Band leads congregation in songs of hope and celebration. Worship leader closes the service. Band reprises "We Danced Anyway" or other exit music.

JOURNEY TO THE CROSS

a Palm Sunday dramatic celebration

Word: Various excerpts from the Gospels
Felt Need: We all face fearful challenges, but God's resurrection power will ultimately prevail.
Desired Outcome: Participants will identify with Jesus and truly experience the journey to the cross.
Theme: Journey to the Cross
Look: Palm branches with a cross in the distance

Throughout the celebration, Gospel readings will be interspersed with drama pieces and excerpts from Max Lucado's retelling of Jesus' challenging journey to the cross. Page numbers are noted for all story excerpts, taken from Max Lucado's book And the Angels Were Silent *(Portland, Ore.: Multnomah Books, 1992).*

In addition to your regular worship personnel, you'll need a guitarist, four readers (they could be vocalists from the worship team), five drama players, and a painter. The drama players should include three adults (two men and a woman), a teenaged girl, and a child. The painter needs to have a large black canvas (approximately six-by-six feet), brushes, and white and red paint.

Opening Song: "Creed" (Rich Mullins)
Opening Words of Story: And the Angels Were Silent, *page 22.*

Call to Worship

"We are going to Jerusalem," he told his disciples. "The Son of Man will be turned over to the leading priests and the teachers of the law, and they will say that he must die. They will give the Son of Man to the . . . people to laugh at him and beat him with whips and crucify him. But on the third day, he will be raised to life again" (Matthew 20:18-19 NCV).

The New Testament Gospel of Matthew details this account: "As they approached Jerusalem and came to Bethphage on the Mount of Olives, Jesus sent two disciples, saying to them, 'Go to the village ahead of you, and at once you will find a donkey tied there, with her colt by her. Untie them and bring them to me. If anyone says anything to you, tell him that the Lord needs them, and he will send them right away.' [Matthew 21:1-3]

"The disciples went and did as Jesus had instructed them. They brought the donkey and the colt, placed their cloaks on them, and Jesus sat on them. A very large crowd spread their cloaks on the road, while others cut branches from the trees and spread them on the road. The crowds that went ahead of him and those that followed shouted, 'Hosanna to the Son of David! Blessed is he who comes in the name of the Lord. Hosanna in the highest!'

"When Jesus entered Jerusalem, the whole city was stirred and asked, 'Who is this?' The crowds answered, 'This is Jesus, the prophet from Nazareth in Galilee.'" [Matthew 21:6-11]

VOCALIST 1: This is the One who was born to die.

VOCALIST 2: This is the One who shows us the way.

VOCALIST 3: This is the One who heals our diseases, who bears our grief, and carries our sorrow.

VOCALIST 4: This is the One we have grown to love . . .

WORSHIP LEADER: The Ancient of Days . . . let's stand and worship together!

Song Celebration

"Ancient of Days" (Jamie Harvill and Gary Sadler); "Glory to Glory to Glory" (Fred Hammond); "Here I Am to Worship" (Tim Hughes)

WORSHIP LEADER: We want to continue giving our best worship to the One who gave so much for us. In a moment we are asking the ushers to come for the offerings we've brought to share. First, hear these next words from Jesus' journey:

Days later while in Jerusalem, one of the teachers of the law came to Jesus and asked him, "Of all the commandments, which is the most important?" "The most important one is this," answered Jesus. "Love the Lord your God with all your heart, soul, mind, and strength."

"Well said, teacher," the man replied. "I believe you are right in saying that we should love God this way. It is more important than all burnt offerings and sacrifices."

When Jesus saw that the man understood, he said to him, "You are not far from the kingdom of God." [adapted from Mark 12:28-34]

Let's worship by giving our offerings now.
The band plays as the offering is collected.

Story of Mary Anointing Jesus

And the Angels Were Silent, pages 48-50.

As the story is read, drama players silently act out the roles of Jesus and Mary.

WORSHIP LEADER: That week, Jesus was in the home of a man known as Simon the leper, a man Jesus had healed. And while he was there, one woman's act of worship was so expensive, so extravagant, it seized the moment entirely . . .

Song (sung by dramatic Mary or another vocalist): "Alabaster Box" (CeCe Winans)

Story: Read the account of the Last Supper from The Message *(Matthew 26:17-37). End the reading just before Jesus' prayer in Gethsemane. As the story is read, display numerous classic art depictions of the Last Supper on screen.*

DRAMATIC JESUS: Father, oh, my Father. Everything is possible with you. I've seen it over and over again. It was you who calmed the sea when they were so afraid. You who brought Lazarus back to life after he'd been gone three days. You parted the Red Sea with your mighty hand. Father, you made a way when they were so afraid. Everything is possible with you. And now, I am the one afraid. I do not want to die the death that is coming . . . except that they need me so much. They need a Savior. They are broken, Father. But if it will heal them, if it will make a way for them to be with us, I will go, Father. I'd do anything for them. (*Pause*) Not my will, but yours be done. (*Jesus bows his head and the lights go down*)

As the band plays "Love Song" (Third Day), the drama players and the painter perform the drama described below.

"Jesus" gets up from his Gethsemane prayer as the guitarist begins playing and singing the song. Jesus walks over to the painter (dressed all

in black) and touches her hands, "commissioning her" to begin painting. She turns to her large black canvas and begins painting a crude Jesus figure on the cross with white paint.

Jesus turns to the first drama scene, a husband and wife bitterly fighting as a young child looks on. The two adults turn away from each other. Jesus reaches down and hugs the child, hugs the mother, and attempts to hug the dad, who is angry and refuses. Jesus, very concerned, then joins mother with child and "blesses" them with a hug. The family freezes in place. Next Jesus goes to a scene where a younger man is talking animatedly on a cell phone. As Jesus comes near, the man apparently receives some very bad news on the phone and slumps down, devastated. Jesus attempts to comfort this man, who is visibly shaken and crying. Seeing that Jesus cares, the man pulls out his wallet and shows him pictures of his family, indicating that the bad news must have been in regard to someone very close. Jesus hugs him and assures him of his presence and care. The man freezes in place.

As Jesus gets up, he is drawn to a third scene, a teenaged girl who is obsessing over her weight (in an imaginary mirror) and then vomits into an imaginary toilet. Jesus pauses and is so taken in by this that he walks to her, lifts up her chin, and in sign language says, "You are beautiful to me." The girl smiles faintly and they touch both hands so as to say that Jesus will be staying in her life. The girl freezes in place.

Jesus slowly turns around to take one last look at each of the drama scenes, then turns and heads back to the painter's canvas. By now the painter has finished the crude "Jesus on the cross" painting with white on black, and has added touches of bright red paint as indication of the blood, pain, and suffering. Jesus steps up on a small stool in front of the canvas and aligns his arms and body with the painted figure, dropping his head as though dying.

One by one, each of the drama players (with the exception of the angry husband, who is still turned away) turns and extends both arms toward Jesus, ending with the painter herself doing the same. Behind all of this, we hear the refrain of the love song: "Just to be with you, I'd do anything . . ."

Slow lighting transition and soft piano music guide the transition toward the following questions (excerpted from And the Angels Were Silent, page 25) delivered by the worship leader.

WORSHIP LEADER: Is there a Jerusalem on your horizon? Are you carrying a heavy cross?

Closing Song: "No Weapon" (Fred Hammond)

(Appropriate closing words of your choosing.)

ARMOR OF GOD FASHION SHOW

dressed for success

Set: Set up a fashion runway in your worship area. Small white Christmas lights work well to mark off the runway.

Actors/Costumes: You'll need a fashion show host and six models. Models should wear clothing similar to the clothing described below, including items that represent the belt of truth, breastplate of righteousness, feet (shoes) fitted with readiness, shield of faith, helmet of salvation, and sword of the Spirit. (We found most of our "armor" at a party costume shop.)

FASHION SHOW HOST: Good evening (morning), ladies and gentlemen. And who wouldn't want to be a sharp dressed man or woman? And so tonight (today), we present to you a magnificent fashion event to challenge the current state of the closet and to consider all-new and improved options for weekend worshipers' wardrobes. Put on these latest accessories, and you're sure to be "dressed for success."

Our first model is Sean, a summer media intern, all dressed up and no place to go! But Sean's tux is no everyday black tie number. Sean is featuring the belt of truth, representing a rock-solid worldview. With this belt in place, the truth about God's purposes in the world becomes amazingly clear. Available in women's sizes as well.

Christopher of Dayton, Ohio, is just in off his Harley, and a fashion statement to behold. Chris sports for us the breastplate of righteousness, a must-have for anyone susceptible to the wind, rain, sleet, and guilt—yes, guilt. For this breastplate carries the declaration that what righteousness we have is in God alone. (Chris makes it easy to believe that!) So if you're out riding and feeling some remorse or need of forgiveness, be sure to nab your own. Comes in silver, gold, or silver and gold.

Now, have you felt a little apprehensive about life? Fearful to take your next steps of faith? Check out these gospel galoshes, feet fitted with readiness of the gospel. Our summer worship intern, Sarah, says they feel oh-so-nice and now looks forward to wherever God takes her, although most days Sarah says, "There's no place like home." (*Model clicks heels three times*) Try these on for size when the future looks bleak and your steps get stuck.

We all know that "stuff happens"—it happens to everyone. But what about when bad things happen to good people? They pull out the shield of faith, guaranteed to ward off stray arrows, harsh criticisms, and the general barrage of day-to-day digs. Erica, recent UD graduate, claims that all people of faith need a shield of their own. Mahvelous, dahling!

A day on the beach can be hard on the hair. What to do to tame those tresses? Matthew, media associate at Ginghamsburg, shares the secret of his success: the helmet of salvation. This headwear not only covers a multitude of bad hair days but also provides a sense of security about just where you stand with God. Just ask Matt. Beach towel and flip flops sold separately.

Lastly, we feature the sword of the Spirit, a slick stick wielding wondrous power, wonder-working power from the word of God. Heidi of Tipp City wants you to know that swords are not just for guys anymore. It's all a matter of putting it to use. The power is in the word—the word of God. Watch it work for you. .

And that's it, ladies and gentlemen. We hope you've been inspired to acquire your own armor of God so you, too, can be dressed for success! Back to you, (Francie) . . .

WORSHIP LEADER: Without the armor of God, we don't have what it takes to fight the good fight. We come today to be challenged to put on whatever it takes to honor Jesus, our Lord and King.